# 50 Bread Recipes for Home

By: Kelly Johnson

## Table of Contents

**Recipes**
- Classic White Bread
- Whole Wheat Bread
- Classic French Baguette
- Classic Italian Focaccia Bread
- Cinnamon Raisin Bread
- Banana Nut Bread
- Garlic and Herb Focaccia
- Whole Grain Seed Bread
- Cinnamon Swirl Bread
- Sun-Dried Tomato and Olive Bread
- Rosemary Garlic Focaccia
- Cheesy Jalapeño Cheddar Bread
- Caramelized Onion and Gruyère Cheese Bread
- Pesto and Sun-Dried Tomato Bread
- Garlic Parmesan Pull-Apart Bread
- **Chocolate Babka**
- Fruity Blueberry Lemon Bread
- Pumpkin Spice Bread
- Cheesy Spinach and Feta Pull-Apart Bread
- Rosemary Olive Oil Bread
- Zucchini Walnut Bread
- Cheesy Jalapeño Cornbread
- Cinnamon Raisin Swirl Bread
- Garlic and Herb Focaccia
- Cherry Almond Bread
- Multigrain Seeded Bread
- Rosemary and Olive No-Knead Bread
- Sun-Dried Tomato and Basil Focaccia
- Cheese and Herb Pull-Apart Bread

- Olive and Rosemary Fougasse
- Challah Bread
- Multigrain Bread
- Cranberry Walnut Bread
- Sun-Dried Tomato and Basil Bread
- Cheese and Herb Filled Pull-Apart Bread
- Caramelized Onion and Gruyère Swirl Bread
- Honey Walnut Whole Wheat Bread
- Rosemary Olive No-Knead Bread
- Cheddar and Jalapeño Artisan Sourdough
- Honey Oat Whole Grain Bread
- Sunflower Seed and Flaxseed Multigrain Bread
- Garlic and Rosemary Fougasse
- Maple Pecan Whole Wheat Bread
- Herb and Onion Focaccia
- Sundried Tomato and Basil Focaccia
- Olive and Herb Ciabatta
- Cheddar and Jalapeño Cornbread
- Cranberry Walnut Artisan Bread
- Rosemary and Garlic No-Knead Bread
- Sunflower Seed Whole Wheat Bread

**Classic White Bread**

Ingredients:

- 4 cups all-purpose flour
- 1 tablespoon sugar
- 1 tablespoon active dry yeast
- 1 teaspoon salt
- 1 1/2 cups warm water (110°F/43°C)
- 2 tablespoons olive oil or vegetable oil

Directions:

Activate the Yeast:
- In a small bowl, combine warm water and sugar. Stir until the sugar dissolves.
- Sprinkle the active dry yeast over the water and let it sit for 5-10 minutes until it becomes frothy.

Mix Dry Ingredients:
- In a large mixing bowl, combine the flour and salt.

Combine Wet and Dry Ingredients:
- Make a well in the center of the flour mixture and pour in the activated yeast mixture.
- Add the olive oil.

Knead the Dough:
- Mix the ingredients until a dough forms.
- Flour a clean surface and knead the dough for about 8-10 minutes, or until it becomes smooth and elastic.

First Rise:
- Place the dough in a lightly oiled bowl, cover it with a clean kitchen towel, and let it rise in a warm place for about 1-2 hours, or until it doubles in size.

Punch Down and Shape:
- Once the dough has risen, punch it down to release the air.
- Shape the dough into a loaf and place it in a greased loaf pan.

Second Rise:
- Cover the loaf with a kitchen towel and let it rise for an additional 30-60 minutes, or until it reaches the top of the pan.

Preheat Oven:
- Preheat your oven to 375°F (190°C).

Bake:

- Bake the bread in the preheated oven for 25-30 minutes, or until the top is golden brown and the bread sounds hollow when tapped.

Cool:
- Allow the bread to cool in the pan for 10 minutes, then transfer it to a wire rack to cool completely before slicing.

Enjoy your freshly baked homemade bread!

**Whole Wheat Bread:**

Ingredients:

- 3 cups whole wheat flour
- 1 cup all-purpose flour
- 1 tablespoon honey
- 1 tablespoon active dry yeast
- 1 1/2 teaspoons salt
- 1 1/4 cups warm water (110°F/43°C)
- 2 tablespoons olive oil

Directions:

Activate the Yeast:
- In a small bowl, combine warm water and honey. Stir until the honey dissolves.
- Sprinkle the active dry yeast over the water and let it sit for 5-10 minutes until it becomes frothy.

Mix Dry Ingredients:
- In a large mixing bowl, combine the whole wheat flour, all-purpose flour, and salt.

Combine Wet and Dry Ingredients:
- Make a well in the center of the flour mixture and pour in the activated yeast mixture.
- Add the olive oil.

Knead the Dough:
- Mix the ingredients until a dough forms.
- Transfer the dough to a floured surface and knead for about 10-12 minutes, or until it becomes smooth and elastic.

First Rise:
- Place the dough in a lightly oiled bowl, cover it with a clean kitchen towel, and let it rise in a warm place for about 1-2 hours, or until it doubles in size.

Punch Down and Shape:
- Once the dough has risen, punch it down to release the air.
- Shape the dough into a loaf and place it in a greased loaf pan.

Second Rise:
- Cover the loaf with a kitchen towel and let it rise for an additional 30-60 minutes, or until it reaches the top of the pan.

Preheat Oven:
- Preheat your oven to 375°F (190°C).

Bake:

- Bake the bread in the preheated oven for 30-35 minutes, or until the top is golden brown and the bread sounds hollow when tapped.

Cool:
- Allow the bread to cool in the pan for 10 minutes, then transfer it to a wire rack to cool completely before slicing.

Enjoy your wholesome whole wheat bread!

**Classic French Baguette:**

Ingredients:

- 4 cups bread flour
- 1 1/2 teaspoons active dry yeast
- 1 1/2 teaspoons salt
- 1 1/4 cups lukewarm water
- 1 tablespoon olive oil (optional, for brushing)

Directions:

> Activate the Yeast:
> - In a small bowl, combine lukewarm water and active dry yeast. Let it sit for about 5-10 minutes until it becomes frothy.
> 
> Mix Dry Ingredients:
> - In a large mixing bowl, combine the bread flour and salt.
> 
> Combine Wet and Dry Ingredients:
> - Make a well in the center of the flour mixture and pour in the activated yeast mixture.
> 
> Knead the Dough:
> - Mix the ingredients until a dough forms.
> - Transfer the dough to a floured surface and knead for about 10 minutes, or until it becomes smooth and elastic.
> 
> First Rise:
> - Place the dough in a lightly oiled bowl, cover it with a clean kitchen towel, and let it rise in a warm place for about 1-2 hours, or until it doubles in size.
> 
> Punch Down and Divide:
> - Once the dough has risen, punch it down to release the air.
> - Divide the dough into two equal portions.
> 
> Shape into Baguettes:
> - Roll each portion into a rectangle and then roll it up tightly from the long side, sealing the seam.
> - Place the shaped baguettes on a parchment-lined baking sheet.
> 
> Second Rise:
> - Cover the baguettes with a kitchen towel and let them rise for an additional 30-45 minutes, or until they visibly expand.
> 
> Preheat Oven:
> - Preheat your oven to 425°F (220°C).
> 
> Score the Baguettes:

- Using a sharp knife or a bread lame, make diagonal slashes along the top of each baguette.

Bake:
- Bake the baguettes in the preheated oven for 20-25 minutes, or until they are golden brown and have a crispy crust.

Optional: Brush with Olive Oil:
- If desired, brush the baked baguettes with olive oil for a shiny finish.

Cool:
- Allow the baguettes to cool on a wire rack for at least 15-20 minutes before slicing.

Enjoy your homemade French baguettes!

**Classic Italian Focaccia Bread:**

Ingredients:

- 4 cups all-purpose flour
- 1 tablespoon sugar
- 2 teaspoons active dry yeast
- 1 1/2 teaspoons salt
- 1 1/2 cups warm water (110°F/43°C)
- 1/4 cup olive oil (plus extra for drizzling)
- Toppings (optional): Rosemary, cherry tomatoes, olives, sea salt

Directions:

Activate the Yeast:
- In a small bowl, combine warm water and sugar. Stir until the sugar dissolves.
- Sprinkle the active dry yeast over the water and let it sit for 5-10 minutes until it becomes frothy.

Mix Dry Ingredients:
- In a large mixing bowl, combine the all-purpose flour and salt.

Combine Wet and Dry Ingredients:
- Make a well in the center of the flour mixture and pour in the activated yeast mixture.
- Add 1/4 cup of olive oil.

Knead the Dough:
- Mix the ingredients until a dough forms.
- Transfer the dough to a floured surface and knead for about 8-10 minutes, or until it becomes smooth and elastic.

First Rise:
- Place the dough in a lightly oiled bowl, cover it with a clean kitchen towel, and let it rise in a warm place for about 1-2 hours, or until it doubles in size.

Prepare Baking Pan:
- Grease a baking sheet or a rectangular baking pan with olive oil.

Shape the Focaccia:
- Transfer the risen dough to the prepared pan and gently press it to cover the pan evenly.
- Use your fingers to create dimples on the surface of the dough.

Second Rise:
- Cover the pan with a kitchen towel and let the dough rise for an additional 30-45 minutes.

Preheat Oven:

- Preheat your oven to 425°F (220°C).

Add Toppings (Optional):
- If desired, press your fingertips into the dough to create more dimples and add toppings like rosemary, cherry tomatoes, olives, or sea salt.

Bake:
- Bake the focaccia in the preheated oven for 20-25 minutes, or until it's golden brown.

Drizzle with Olive Oil:
- Once out of the oven, drizzle the top of the focaccia with some extra olive oil.

Cool:
- Allow the focaccia to cool slightly before slicing and serving.

**Cinnamon Raisin Bread:**

Ingredients:

- 1 1/2 cups warm milk (110°F/43°C)
- 1/4 cup unsalted butter, melted
- 1/4 cup granulated sugar
- 1 tablespoon active dry yeast
- 4 cups all-purpose flour
- 1 teaspoon salt
- 1 1/2 teaspoons ground cinnamon
- 1 cup raisins

For the Cinnamon-Sugar Filling:

- 1/4 cup unsalted butter, softened
- 1/2 cup brown sugar
- 2 teaspoons ground cinnamon

Directions:

Activate the Yeast:
- In a bowl, combine warm milk, melted butter, and sugar. Stir until the sugar dissolves.
- Sprinkle the active dry yeast over the mixture and let it sit for 5-10 minutes until it becomes frothy.

Mix Dry Ingredients:
- In a large mixing bowl, combine the all-purpose flour, salt, and ground cinnamon.

Combine Wet and Dry Ingredients:
- Make a well in the center of the flour mixture and pour in the activated yeast mixture.
- Mix until a dough forms.

Knead the Dough:
- Transfer the dough to a floured surface and knead for about 8-10 minutes, or until it becomes smooth and elastic.

First Rise:
- Place the dough in a lightly oiled bowl, cover it with a clean kitchen towel, and let it rise in a warm place for about 1-2 hours, or until it doubles in size.

Prepare Filling:
- In a small bowl, mix together the softened butter, brown sugar, and ground cinnamon to create the filling.

Roll and Fill:
- Punch down the risen dough and roll it out into a rectangle.
- Spread the cinnamon-sugar filling evenly over the dough.
- Sprinkle raisins evenly over the filling.

Shape and Second Rise:
- Roll up the dough tightly from the long side to form a log.
- Place the rolled dough in a greased loaf pan.
- Cover with a kitchen towel and let it rise for an additional 30-45 minutes.

Preheat Oven:
- Preheat your oven to 350°F (175°C).

Bake:
- Bake the cinnamon raisin bread in the preheated oven for 30-35 minutes, or until it's golden brown and sounds hollow when tapped.

Cool:
- Allow the bread to cool in the pan for 10 minutes, then transfer it to a wire rack to cool completely before slicing.

Enjoy your delicious homemade Cinnamon Raisin Bread! It's perfect for toasting, making French toast, or simply enjoying with a spread of butter.

**Banana Nut Bread:**

Ingredients:

- 2 to 3 ripe bananas, mashed
- 1 teaspoon lemon juice (to prevent bananas from browning)
- 1/2 cup unsalted butter, melted
- 1 cup granulated sugar
- 2 large eggs
- 1 teaspoon vanilla extract
- 1 3/4 cups all-purpose flour
- 1 teaspoon baking soda
- 1/2 teaspoon salt
- 1/2 teaspoon ground cinnamon
- 1/2 cup chopped nuts (walnuts or pecans), optional

Directions:

Preheat Oven:
- Preheat your oven to 350°F (175°C). Grease a 9x5-inch loaf pan.

Mash Bananas:
- In a small bowl, mash the ripe bananas with lemon juice. Set aside.

Mix Wet Ingredients:
- In a large mixing bowl, combine melted butter and sugar. Stir until well combined.
- Add the eggs one at a time, beating well after each addition.
- Stir in the mashed bananas and vanilla extract.

Mix Dry Ingredients:
- In a separate bowl, whisk together the flour, baking soda, salt, and ground cinnamon.

Combine Wet and Dry Ingredients:
- Add the dry ingredients to the wet ingredients, stirring just until combined. Be careful not to overmix.
- If using, fold in the chopped nuts.

Pour into Pan:
- Pour the batter into the greased loaf pan.

Bake:
- Bake in the preheated oven for 60-70 minutes or until a toothpick inserted into the center comes out clean or with a few moist crumbs.

Cool:

- Allow the banana nut bread to cool in the pan for about 10 minutes, then transfer it to a wire rack to cool completely.

Slice and Serve:
- Once cooled, slice the banana nut bread and serve. It's delicious on its own or with a smear of butter.

Enjoy your homemade Banana Nut Bread!

**Garlic and Herb Focaccia:**

Ingredients:

For the Dough:

- 4 cups all-purpose flour
- 1 tablespoon sugar
- 1 tablespoon active dry yeast
- 1 1/2 teaspoons salt
- 1 1/2 cups warm water (110°F/43°C)
- 1/4 cup olive oil

For the Topping:

- 1/4 cup olive oil
- 4 cloves garlic, minced
- 1 tablespoon fresh rosemary, chopped
- 1 tablespoon fresh thyme leaves
- 1 teaspoon sea salt (for sprinkling)

Directions:

Activate the Yeast:
- In a small bowl, combine warm water and sugar. Stir until the sugar dissolves.
- Sprinkle the active dry yeast over the water and let it sit for 5-10 minutes until it becomes frothy.

Mix Dry Ingredients:
- In a large mixing bowl, combine the all-purpose flour and salt.

Combine Wet and Dry Ingredients:
- Make a well in the center of the flour mixture and pour in the activated yeast mixture.
- Add 1/4 cup of olive oil.
- Mix until a dough forms.

Knead the Dough:
- Transfer the dough to a floured surface and knead for about 8-10 minutes, or until it becomes smooth and elastic.

First Rise:
- Place the dough in a lightly oiled bowl, cover it with a clean kitchen towel, and let it rise in a warm place for about 1-2 hours, or until it doubles in size.

Prepare Topping:

- In a small saucepan, heat 1/4 cup of olive oil over medium heat.
- Add minced garlic and cook for 1-2 minutes until fragrant. Remove from heat.
- Stir in chopped rosemary and thyme.

Preheat Oven:
- Preheat your oven to 425°F (220°C).

Shape and Second Rise:
- Punch down the risen dough and transfer it to a greased baking sheet.
- Press the dough evenly onto the baking sheet.
- Cover with a kitchen towel and let it rise for an additional 30 minutes.

Create Indentations:
- Use your fingers to create deep indentations in the dough.

Add Topping:
- Brush the garlic and herb mixture evenly over the surface of the dough.
- Sprinkle sea salt over the top.

Bake:
- Bake in the preheated oven for 20-25 minutes, or until the focaccia is golden brown.

Cool:
- Allow the focaccia to cool slightly before slicing.

Serve this Garlic and Herb Focaccia as a side to your favorite Italian dishes, or enjoy it on its own with a drizzle of olive oil. It's perfect for sharing!

**Whole Grain Seed Bread:**

Ingredients:

For the Bread:

- 2 cups whole wheat flour
- 1 cup all-purpose flour
- 1/2 cup rolled oats
- 1/4 cup flaxseeds, ground
- 1/4 cup sunflower seeds
- 1/4 cup pumpkin seeds
- 1/4 cup sesame seeds
- 1 tablespoon active dry yeast
- 1 1/2 teaspoons salt
- 1 1/2 cups warm water (110°F/43°C)
- 2 tablespoons honey or maple syrup
- 2 tablespoons olive oil

For Topping:

- Additional seeds for sprinkling (sunflower, pumpkin, sesame, etc.)

Directions:

Activate the Yeast:
- In a bowl, combine warm water and honey or maple syrup. Stir until the sweetener dissolves.

- Sprinkle the active dry yeast over the water and let it sit for 5-10 minutes until it becomes frothy.

Mix Dry Ingredients:
- In a large mixing bowl, combine whole wheat flour, all-purpose flour, rolled oats, ground flaxseeds, sunflower seeds, pumpkin seeds, sesame seeds, and salt.

Combine Wet and Dry Ingredients:
- Make a well in the center of the flour mixture and pour in the activated yeast mixture.
- Add olive oil.
- Mix until a dough forms.

Knead the Dough:
- Transfer the dough to a floured surface and knead for about 10 minutes, or until it becomes smooth and elastic.

First Rise:
- Place the dough in a lightly oiled bowl, cover it with a clean kitchen towel, and let it rise in a warm place for about 1-2 hours, or until it doubles in size.

Shape the Loaf:
- Punch down the risen dough and shape it into a loaf.
- Place the shaped dough in a greased loaf pan.

Second Rise:
- Cover the loaf with a kitchen towel and let it rise for an additional 30-45 minutes, or until it reaches the top of the pan.

Preheat Oven:
- Preheat your oven to 375°F (190°C).

Brush with Water and Add Seeds:
- Lightly brush the top of the loaf with water.
- Sprinkle additional seeds on top for a decorative and crunchy crust.

Bake:

- Bake the bread in the preheated oven for 30-40 minutes, or until it's golden brown and sounds hollow when tapped.

Cool:

- Allow the bread to cool in the pan for 10 minutes, then transfer it to a wire rack to cool completely before slicing.

Enjoy your wholesome Whole Grain Seed Bread! This bread is packed with nutrients and the combination of seeds adds a delightful crunch. It's great for sandwiches or simply toasted with butter.

**Cinnamon Swirl Bread:**

Ingredients:

For the Dough:

- 3 1/4 cups all-purpose flour
- 1/4 cup granulated sugar
- 1 teaspoon salt
- 1 tablespoon active dry yeast
- 1 cup warm milk (110°F/43°C)
- 2 tablespoons unsalted butter, melted
- 1 large egg

For the Filling:

- 1/2 cup granulated sugar
- 2 tablespoons ground cinnamon
- 3 tablespoons unsalted butter, softened

For the Glaze (Optional):

- 1 cup powdered sugar
- 2 tablespoons milk
- 1/2 teaspoon vanilla extract

Directions:

Activate the Yeast:

- In a small bowl, combine warm milk and 1 tablespoon of sugar. Stir until the sugar dissolves.
- Sprinkle the active dry yeast over the milk mixture and let it sit for 5-10 minutes until it becomes frothy.

Prepare the Dough:

- In a large mixing bowl, combine 3 cups of flour, remaining sugar, and salt.
- Add the activated yeast mixture, melted butter, and egg to the flour mixture.
- Mix until a soft dough forms.

Knead the Dough:

- Transfer the dough to a floured surface and knead for about 8-10 minutes, or until it becomes smooth and elastic. Add more flour if needed.

First Rise:

- Place the dough in a lightly oiled bowl, cover it with a clean kitchen towel, and let it rise in a warm place for about 1-2 hours, or until it doubles in size.

Prepare the Filling:

- In a small bowl, mix together the sugar and ground cinnamon for the filling.

Shape and Fill:

- Punch down the risen dough and roll it out into a rectangle.
- Spread the softened butter over the dough, leaving a small border around the edges.
- Sprinkle the cinnamon-sugar mixture evenly over the butter.

Roll and Second Rise:

- Roll up the dough tightly from the long side to form a log.
- Place the rolled dough in a greased loaf pan.
- Cover with a kitchen towel and let it rise for an additional 30-45 minutes.

Preheat Oven:

- Preheat your oven to 350°F (175°C).

Bake:

- Bake the cinnamon swirl bread in the preheated oven for 30-35 minutes, or until it's golden brown and sounds hollow when tapped.

Optional Glaze:

- If desired, whisk together powdered sugar, milk, and vanilla extract to make a glaze. Drizzle the glaze over the cooled bread.

Cool:

- Allow the bread to cool in the pan for 10 minutes, then transfer it to a wire rack to cool completely before slicing.

Enjoy your homemade Cinnamon Swirl Bread! It's perfect for breakfast or as a sweet treat any time of the day.

**Sun-Dried Tomato and Olive Bread:**

Ingredients:

For the Dough:

- 3 cups all-purpose flour
- 1 tablespoon sugar
- 1 tablespoon active dry yeast
- 1 1/2 teaspoons salt
- 1 cup warm water (110°F/43°C)
- 2 tablespoons olive oil

For the Filling:

- 1/2 cup sun-dried tomatoes, chopped
- 1/2 cup black olives, pitted and chopped
- 1/4 cup fresh basil, chopped
- 1/4 cup feta cheese, crumbled (optional)
- 2 tablespoons olive oil

For Topping:

- 1 tablespoon sesame seeds
- 1 tablespoon dried oregano

Directions:

Activate the Yeast:
- In a small bowl, combine warm water and sugar. Stir until the sugar dissolves.

- Sprinkle the active dry yeast over the water and let it sit for 5-10 minutes until it becomes frothy.

Prepare the Dough:
- In a large mixing bowl, combine flour and salt.
- Add the activated yeast mixture and olive oil to the flour.
- Mix until a dough forms.

Knead the Dough:
- Transfer the dough to a floured surface and knead for about 8-10 minutes, or until it becomes smooth and elastic.

First Rise:
- Place the dough in a lightly oiled bowl, cover it with a clean kitchen towel, and let it rise in a warm place for about 1-2 hours, or until it doubles in size.

Prepare the Filling:
- In a small bowl, combine chopped sun-dried tomatoes, chopped olives, chopped fresh basil, and crumbled feta cheese (if using).
- Drizzle 2 tablespoons of olive oil over the mixture and toss until well combined.

Shape the Bread:
- Punch down the risen dough and roll it out into a rectangle.
- Spread the sun-dried tomato and olive mixture evenly over the dough.

Roll and Second Rise:
- Roll up the dough tightly from the long side to form a log.
- Place the rolled dough in a greased loaf pan.
- Cover with a kitchen towel and let it rise for an additional 30-45 minutes.

Preheat Oven:
- Preheat your oven to 375°F (190°C).

Topping:

- Brush the top of the risen loaf with water and sprinkle sesame seeds and dried oregano over the surface.

Bake:

- Bake the bread in the preheated oven for 30-35 minutes, or until it's golden brown and sounds hollow when tapped.

Cool:

- Allow the bread to cool in the pan for 10 minutes, then transfer it to a wire rack to cool completely before slicing.

Enjoy your flavorful Sun-Dried Tomato and Olive Bread! It's a wonderful combination of savory ingredients that makes for a delicious and unique loaf.

**Rosemary Garlic Focaccia:**

Ingredients:

For the Dough:

- 4 cups all-purpose flour
- 1 tablespoon sugar
- 1 tablespoon active dry yeast
- 1 1/2 teaspoons salt
- 1 1/2 cups warm water (110°F/43°C)
- 1/4 cup olive oil

For the Topping:

- 3 tablespoons olive oil
- 3 cloves garlic, minced
- 1 tablespoon fresh rosemary, chopped
- Sea salt, for sprinkling

Directions:

Activate the Yeast:
- In a small bowl, combine warm water and sugar. Stir until the sugar dissolves.
- Sprinkle the active dry yeast over the water and let it sit for 5-10 minutes until it becomes frothy.

Mix the Dough:
- In a large mixing bowl, combine the all-purpose flour and salt.
- Make a well in the center and pour in the activated yeast mixture and olive oil.

- Mix until a dough forms.

Knead the Dough:

- Transfer the dough to a floured surface and knead for about 8-10 minutes, or until it becomes smooth and elastic.

First Rise:

- Place the dough in a lightly oiled bowl, cover it with a clean kitchen towel, and let it rise in a warm place for about 1-2 hours, or until it doubles in size.

Prepare the Topping:

- In a small saucepan, heat 3 tablespoons of olive oil over medium heat.
- Add minced garlic and chopped rosemary. Cook for 1-2 minutes until fragrant. Remove from heat.

Shape the Focaccia:

- Punch down the risen dough and transfer it to a greased baking sheet.
- Press the dough evenly onto the baking sheet.
- Use your fingers to create dimples in the dough.

Second Rise:

- Cover the shaped dough with a kitchen towel and let it rise for an additional 30-45 minutes.

Preheat Oven:

- Preheat your oven to 425°F (220°C).

Add Topping:

- Drizzle the garlic and rosemary mixture evenly over the surface of the dough.
- Sprinkle sea salt over the top.

Bake:

- Bake the focaccia in the preheated oven for 20-25 minutes, or until it's golden brown.

Cool:

- Allow the focaccia to cool slightly before slicing.

Enjoy your homemade Rosemary Garlic Focaccia! This bread is wonderfully aromatic and makes a fantastic accompaniment to soups, salads, or as a tasty appetizer.

**Cheesy Jalapeño Cheddar Bread:**

Ingredients:

For the Dough:

- 4 cups all-purpose flour
- 1 tablespoon sugar
- 1 tablespoon active dry yeast
- 1 1/2 teaspoons salt
- 1 1/2 cups warm water (110°F/43°C)
- 2 tablespoons olive oil

For the Filling:

- 1 cup sharp cheddar cheese, shredded
- 2-3 fresh jalapeños, seeded and finely chopped
- 1/4 cup green onions, chopped

For Topping:

- 1/2 cup sharp cheddar cheese, shredded
- Sliced jalapeños and green onions for garnish

Directions:

Activate the Yeast:
- In a small bowl, combine warm water and sugar. Stir until the sugar dissolves.
- Sprinkle the active dry yeast over the water and let it sit for 5-10 minutes until it becomes frothy.

Mix the Dough:

- In a large mixing bowl, combine the all-purpose flour and salt.
- Make a well in the center and pour in the activated yeast mixture and olive oil.
- Mix until a dough forms.

Knead the Dough:

- Transfer the dough to a floured surface and knead for about 8-10 minutes, or until it becomes smooth and elastic.

First Rise:

- Place the dough in a lightly oiled bowl, cover it with a clean kitchen towel, and let it rise in a warm place for about 1-2 hours, or until it doubles in size.

Prepare the Filling:

- In a bowl, mix together shredded cheddar cheese, chopped jalapeños, and green onions.

Shape the Bread:

- Punch down the risen dough and roll it out into a rectangle.
- Spread the jalapeño and cheddar filling evenly over the dough.

Roll and Second Rise:

- Roll up the dough tightly from the long side to form a log.
- Place the rolled dough in a greased loaf pan.
- Cover with a kitchen towel and let it rise for an additional 30-45 minutes.

Preheat Oven:

- Preheat your oven to 375°F (190°C).

Add Topping:

- Sprinkle additional shredded cheddar cheese on top of the risen dough.
- Garnish with sliced jalapeños and green onions.

Bake:

- Bake the bread in the preheated oven for 30-35 minutes, or until it's golden brown and sounds hollow when tapped.

Cool:

- Allow the bread to cool in the pan for 10 minutes, then transfer it to a wire rack to cool completely before slicing.

Enjoy your homemade Jalapeño Cheddar Bread! It's a savory and spicy treat that's perfect for serving as a snack or alongside your favorite soups and chili.

**Caramelized Onion and Gruyère Cheese Bread:**

Ingredients:

For the Dough:

- 4 cups all-purpose flour
- 1 tablespoon sugar
- 1 tablespoon active dry yeast
- 1 1/2 teaspoons salt
- 1 1/2 cups warm water (110°F/43°C)
- 2 tablespoons olive oil

For the Filling:

- 2 large onions, thinly sliced
- 2 tablespoons unsalted butter
- 1 teaspoon sugar
- 1 cup Gruyère cheese, grated
- Salt and pepper to taste
- Fresh thyme leaves for garnish (optional)

Directions:

Activate the Yeast:
- In a small bowl, combine warm water and sugar. Stir until the sugar dissolves.
- Sprinkle the active dry yeast over the water and let it sit for 5-10 minutes until it becomes frothy.

Mix the Dough:

- In a large mixing bowl, combine the all-purpose flour and salt.
- Make a well in the center and pour in the activated yeast mixture and olive oil.
- Mix until a dough forms.

Knead the Dough:

- Transfer the dough to a floured surface and knead for about 8-10 minutes, or until it becomes smooth and elastic.

First Rise:

- Place the dough in a lightly oiled bowl, cover it with a clean kitchen towel, and let it rise in a warm place for about 1-2 hours, or until it doubles in size.

Prepare the Filling:

- In a skillet, melt butter over medium heat.
- Add thinly sliced onions and sugar to the skillet and cook, stirring occasionally, until the onions are caramelized and golden brown. Season with salt and pepper.
- Allow the caramelized onions to cool.

Shape the Bread:

- Punch down the risen dough and roll it out into a rectangle.
- Spread the caramelized onions evenly over the dough.
- Sprinkle grated Gruyère cheese over the onions.

Roll and Second Rise:

- Roll up the dough tightly from the long side to form a log.
- Place the rolled dough in a greased loaf pan.
- Cover with a kitchen towel and let it rise for an additional 30-45 minutes.

Preheat Oven:

- Preheat your oven to 375°F (190°C).

Bake:

- Bake the bread in the preheated oven for 30-35 minutes, or until it's golden brown and sounds hollow when tapped.

Cool:

- Allow the bread to cool in the pan for 10 minutes, then transfer it to a wire rack to cool completely before slicing.

Garnish:

- Optionally, garnish the top with fresh thyme leaves for added flavor and a decorative touch.

Enjoy your homemade Caramelized Onion and Gruyère Cheese Bread! This bread is rich, savory, and perfect for serving as an appetizer or as a complement to a cheese platter.

**Pesto and Sun-Dried Tomato Bread:**

Ingredients:

For the Dough:

- 4 cups all-purpose flour
- 1 tablespoon sugar
- 1 tablespoon active dry yeast
- 1 1/2 teaspoons salt
- 1 1/2 cups warm water (110°F/43°C)
- 2 tablespoons olive oil

For the Filling:

- 1/2 cup basil pesto
- 1/2 cup sun-dried tomatoes, chopped
- 1/2 cup Parmesan cheese, grated
- Fresh basil leaves for garnish (optional)

Directions:

Activate the Yeast:
- In a small bowl, combine warm water and sugar. Stir until the sugar dissolves.
- Sprinkle the active dry yeast over the water and let it sit for 5-10 minutes until it becomes frothy.

Mix the Dough:
- In a large mixing bowl, combine the all-purpose flour and salt.
- Make a well in the center and pour in the activated yeast mixture and olive oil.

- Mix until a dough forms.

Knead the Dough:

- Transfer the dough to a floured surface and knead for about 8-10 minutes, or until it becomes smooth and elastic.

First Rise:

- Place the dough in a lightly oiled bowl, cover it with a clean kitchen towel, and let it rise in a warm place for about 1-2 hours, or until it doubles in size.

Prepare the Filling:

- In a small bowl, mix together basil pesto, chopped sun-dried tomatoes, and grated Parmesan cheese.

Shape the Bread:

- Punch down the risen dough and roll it out into a rectangle.
- Spread the pesto and sun-dried tomato mixture evenly over the dough.

Roll and Second Rise:

- Roll up the dough tightly from the long side to form a log.
- Place the rolled dough in a greased loaf pan.
- Cover with a kitchen towel and let it rise for an additional 30-45 minutes.

Preheat Oven:

- Preheat your oven to 375°F (190°C).

Bake:

- Bake the bread in the preheated oven for 30-35 minutes, or until it's golden brown and sounds hollow when tapped.

Cool:

- Allow the bread to cool in the pan for 10 minutes, then transfer it to a wire rack to cool completely before slicing.

Garnish:

- Optionally, garnish the top with fresh basil leaves for added freshness and flavor.

Enjoy your homemade Pesto and Sun-Dried Tomato Bread! This bread is bursting with Mediterranean flavors and is perfect for serving alongside soups, salads, or as a delicious snack.

**Garlic Parmesan Pull-Apart Bread:**

Ingredients:

For the Dough:

- 4 cups all-purpose flour
- 1 tablespoon sugar
- 1 tablespoon active dry yeast
- 1 1/2 teaspoons salt
- 1 cup warm milk (110°F/43°C)
- 1/4 cup unsalted butter, melted
- 2 tablespoons olive oil

For the Filling:

- 1/2 cup unsalted butter, softened
- 4 cloves garlic, minced
- 1/4 cup fresh parsley, chopped
- 1 cup Parmesan cheese, grated

For Topping:

- Additional grated Parmesan cheese
- Fresh parsley, chopped

Directions:

Activate the Yeast:

- In a small bowl, combine warm milk and sugar. Stir until the sugar dissolves.

- Sprinkle the active dry yeast over the milk and let it sit for 5-10 minutes until it becomes frothy.

Mix the Dough:
- In a large mixing bowl, combine the all-purpose flour, salt, melted butter, and olive oil.
- Make a well in the center and pour in the activated yeast mixture.
- Mix until a dough forms.

Knead the Dough:
- Transfer the dough to a floured surface and knead for about 8-10 minutes, or until it becomes smooth and elastic.

First Rise:
- Place the dough in a lightly oiled bowl, cover it with a clean kitchen towel, and let it rise in a warm place for about 1-2 hours, or until it doubles in size.

Prepare the Filling:
- In a small bowl, mix together softened butter, minced garlic, chopped parsley, and grated Parmesan cheese.

Shape the Bread:
- Punch down the risen dough and roll it out into a rectangle.
- Spread the garlic Parmesan mixture evenly over the dough.

Cut and Stack:
- Using a sharp knife or a pizza cutter, cut the dough into squares.
- Stack the squares on top of each other to form a layered stack.

Place in Loaf Pan:
- Carefully transfer the stacked dough squares into a greased loaf pan.

Second Rise:
- Cover the loaf pan with a kitchen towel and let it rise for an additional 30-45 minutes.

Preheat Oven:
- Preheat your oven to 375°F (190°C).

Topping:
- Sprinkle additional grated Parmesan cheese and chopped fresh parsley over the top of the stacked dough.

Bake:
- Bake the bread in the preheated oven for 25-30 minutes, or until it's golden brown and sounds hollow when tapped.

Cool:
- Allow the bread to cool in the pan for 10 minutes, then transfer it to a wire rack to cool completely before pulling apart and serving.

Enjoy your Garlic Parmesan Pull-Apart Bread! This bread is not only delicious but also fun to pull apart and share. It's perfect for gatherings or as a flavorful side dish.

**Chocolate Babka:**

Ingredients:

For the Dough:

- 4 cups all-purpose flour
- 1/3 cup granulated sugar
- 1 tablespoon active dry yeast
- 1 teaspoon salt
- 1 cup warm milk (110°F/43°C)
- 1/2 cup unsalted butter, softened
- 2 large eggs

For the Filling:

- 1 cup semi-sweet chocolate chips or chopped chocolate
- 1/2 cup unsalted butter
- 1/2 cup granulated sugar
- 3 tablespoons unsweetened cocoa powder
- 1 teaspoon ground cinnamon

For the Syrup:

- 1/4 cup water
- 1/4 cup granulated sugar

Directions:

Activate the Yeast:
- In a small bowl, combine warm milk and 1 tablespoon of sugar. Stir until the sugar dissolves.
- Sprinkle the active dry yeast over the milk and let it sit for 5-10 minutes until it becomes frothy.

Mix the Dough:
- In a large mixing bowl, combine the all-purpose flour, remaining sugar, and salt.
- Make a well in the center and pour in the activated yeast mixture, softened butter, and eggs.

- Mix until a dough forms.

Knead the Dough:
- Transfer the dough to a floured surface and knead for about 8-10 minutes, or until it becomes smooth and elastic.

First Rise:
- Place the dough in a lightly oiled bowl, cover it with a clean kitchen towel, and let it rise in a warm place for about 1-2 hours, or until it doubles in size.

Prepare the Filling:
- In a saucepan, melt the butter for the filling over medium heat.
- Stir in chocolate, sugar, cocoa powder, and ground cinnamon until well combined. Remove from heat and let it cool.

Roll and Fill:
- Roll out the risen dough on a floured surface into a large rectangle.
- Spread the chocolate filling evenly over the dough.

Shape the Babka:
- Roll the dough tightly from the long side to form a log.
- Cut the log in half lengthwise to expose the layers.
- Twist the two halves around each other to form a braided loaf.

Place in Loaf Pan:
- Transfer the twisted dough into a greased loaf pan.

Second Rise:
- Cover the loaf pan with a kitchen towel and let it rise for an additional 30-45 minutes.

Preheat Oven:
- Preheat your oven to 350°F (175°C).

Bake:
- Bake the Chocolate Babka in the preheated oven for 25-30 minutes, or until it's golden brown and sounds hollow when tapped.

Prepare the Syrup:
- In a small saucepan, combine water and sugar for the syrup. Heat over medium heat until the sugar dissolves. Remove from heat.

Syrup and Cool:
- Once the Babka is out of the oven, brush the syrup over the top while it's still warm.
- Allow the Chocolate Babka to cool in the pan for 10 minutes, then transfer it to a wire rack to cool completely before slicing.

Enjoy your homemade Chocolate Babka! This sweet and twisted bread is perfect for breakfast or as a delightful dessert.

**Fruity Blueberry Lemon Bread:**

Ingredients:

For the Bread:

- 2 cups all-purpose flour
- 1 teaspoon baking powder
- 1/2 teaspoon baking soda
- 1/2 teaspoon salt
- 1/2 cup unsalted butter, softened
- 1 cup granulated sugar
- 2 large eggs
- 1 cup plain Greek yogurt
- Zest of 1 lemon
- 1 tablespoon lemon juice
- 1 teaspoon vanilla extract
- 1 1/2 cups fresh blueberries

For the Lemon Glaze:

- 1 cup powdered sugar
- 2 tablespoons fresh lemon juice
- Zest of 1 lemon

Directions:

Preheat Oven:
- Preheat your oven to 350°F (175°C). Grease and flour a 9x5-inch loaf pan.

Mix Dry Ingredients:
- In a medium bowl, whisk together the flour, baking powder, baking soda, and salt. Set aside.

Cream Butter and Sugar:
- In a large mixing bowl, cream together the softened butter and granulated sugar until light and fluffy.

Add Eggs and Flavorings:
- Add the eggs one at a time, beating well after each addition.
- Mix in the lemon zest, lemon juice, and vanilla extract.

Alternate Dry Ingredients and Yogurt:

- Gradually add the dry ingredients to the wet ingredients, alternating with the Greek yogurt. Begin and end with the dry ingredients. Mix until just combined.

Fold in Blueberries:
- Gently fold in the fresh blueberries until evenly distributed in the batter.

Bake:
- Pour the batter into the prepared loaf pan.
- Bake in the preheated oven for 50-60 minutes or until a toothpick inserted into the center comes out clean.

Cool:
- Allow the bread to cool in the pan for 10 minutes, then transfer it to a wire rack to cool completely.

Prepare Lemon Glaze:
- In a small bowl, whisk together powdered sugar, fresh lemon juice, and lemon zest to make the glaze.

Glaze the Bread:
- Once the bread has cooled, drizzle the lemon glaze over the top.

Slice and Serve:
- Allow the glaze to set before slicing. Slice and serve the Blueberry Lemon Bread.

Enjoy your Blueberry Lemon Bread with a burst of fruity flavor and a zesty lemon kick! It's perfect for breakfast, brunch, or as a delightful dessert.

**Pumpkin Spice Bread:**

Ingredients:

For the Bread:

- 2 cups all-purpose flour
- 1 teaspoon baking soda
- 1/2 teaspoon baking powder
- 1/2 teaspoon salt
- 1 teaspoon ground cinnamon
- 1/2 teaspoon ground nutmeg
- 1/4 teaspoon ground cloves
- 1/4 teaspoon ground ginger
- 1/2 cup unsalted butter, softened
- 1 cup granulated sugar
- 2 large eggs
- 1 cup canned pumpkin puree
- 1/4 cup plain Greek yogurt or sour cream
- 1 teaspoon vanilla extract

For the Cream Cheese Frosting:

- 8 oz (225g) cream cheese, softened
- 1/4 cup unsalted butter, softened
- 2 cups powdered sugar
- 1 teaspoon vanilla extract

Directions:

Preheat Oven:
- Preheat your oven to 350°F (175°C). Grease and flour a 9x5-inch loaf pan.

Mix Dry Ingredients:
- In a medium bowl, whisk together the flour, baking soda, baking powder, salt, cinnamon, nutmeg, cloves, and ginger. Set aside.

Cream Butter and Sugar:
- In a large mixing bowl, cream together the softened butter and granulated sugar until light and fluffy.

Add Eggs and Pumpkin:
- Add the eggs one at a time, beating well after each addition.

- Mix in the canned pumpkin puree, Greek yogurt (or sour cream), and vanilla extract until well combined.

Incorporate Dry Ingredients:
- Gradually add the dry ingredients to the wet ingredients, mixing until just combined. Do not overmix.

Pour into Loaf Pan:
- Pour the batter into the prepared loaf pan, spreading it evenly.

Bake:
- Bake in the preheated oven for 60-70 minutes, or until a toothpick inserted into the center comes out clean. If the top is browning too quickly, you can loosely cover it with aluminum foil.

Cool:
- Allow the Pumpkin Spice Bread to cool in the pan for about 10 minutes, then transfer it to a wire rack to cool completely.

Prepare Cream Cheese Frosting:
- In a mixing bowl, beat together the softened cream cheese, softened butter, powdered sugar, and vanilla extract until smooth and creamy.

Frost the Bread:
- Once the bread is completely cooled, spread the cream cheese frosting over the top.

Slice and Serve:
- Slice the Pumpkin Spice Bread into thick slices and serve.

Enjoy your homemade Pumpkin Spice Bread with cream cheese frosting! This seasonal treat is perfect for fall and is sure to be a hit with its warm and comforting flavors.

**Cheesy Spinach and Feta Pull-Apart Bread:**

Ingredients:

For the Dough:

- 4 cups all-purpose flour
- 1 tablespoon sugar
- 1 tablespoon active dry yeast
- 1 1/2 teaspoons salt
- 1 1/2 cups warm water (110°F/43°C)
- 2 tablespoons olive oil

For the Filling:

- 2 cups fresh spinach, chopped
- 1 cup feta cheese, crumbled
- 1/2 cup grated Parmesan cheese
- 4 cloves garlic, minced
- 2 tablespoons olive oil
- Salt and pepper to taste

For Topping:

- 1/4 cup melted butter
- 1 tablespoon chopped fresh parsley

Directions:

Activate the Yeast:
- In a small bowl, combine warm water and sugar. Stir until the sugar dissolves.
- Sprinkle the active dry yeast over the water and let it sit for 5-10 minutes until it becomes frothy.

Mix the Dough:
- In a large mixing bowl, combine the all-purpose flour and salt.
- Make a well in the center and pour in the activated yeast mixture and olive oil.
- Mix until a dough forms.

Knead the Dough:
- Transfer the dough to a floured surface and knead for about 8-10 minutes, or until it becomes smooth and elastic.

First Rise:

- Place the dough in a lightly oiled bowl, cover it with a clean kitchen towel, and let it rise in a warm place for about 1-2 hours, or until it doubles in size.

Prepare the Filling:
- In a skillet, heat 2 tablespoons of olive oil over medium heat.
- Add minced garlic and chopped spinach. Cook until the spinach wilts.
- Remove from heat and let it cool.
- In a bowl, combine the cooked spinach and garlic with crumbled feta and grated Parmesan. Season with salt and pepper.

Shape the Bread:
- Punch down the risen dough and roll it out into a large rectangle.
- Spread the spinach and feta mixture evenly over the dough.

Roll and Second Rise:
- Roll up the dough tightly from the long side to form a log.
- Cut the log into smaller sections (about 2 inches each) to create individual rolls.
- Place the rolls in a greased baking dish.
- Cover with a kitchen towel and let it rise for an additional 30-45 minutes.

Preheat Oven:
- Preheat your oven to 375°F (190°C).

Brush with Butter:
- Brush the melted butter over the top of the risen rolls.

Bake:
- Bake the pull-apart bread in the preheated oven for 25-30 minutes, or until it's golden brown.

Garnish:
- Sprinkle chopped fresh parsley over the top before serving.

Enjoy your homemade Spinach and Feta Pull-Apart Bread! This savory and cheesy bread is perfect for sharing and makes a fantastic appetizer or side dish.

**Rosemary Olive Oil Bread:**

Ingredients:

For the Dough:

- 4 cups bread flour
- 1 tablespoon sugar
- 1 tablespoon active dry yeast
- 1 1/2 teaspoons salt
- 1 1/4 cups warm water (110°F/43°C)
- 3 tablespoons olive oil
- 1 tablespoon fresh rosemary, finely chopped

For Topping:

- 2 tablespoons olive oil
- 1 tablespoon fresh rosemary, chopped
- Sea salt for sprinkling

Directions:

Activate the Yeast:
- In a small bowl, combine warm water and sugar. Stir until the sugar dissolves.
- Sprinkle the active dry yeast over the water and let it sit for 5-10 minutes until it becomes frothy.

Mix the Dough:
- In a large mixing bowl, combine bread flour and salt.
- Make a well in the center and pour in the activated yeast mixture and olive oil.
- Add the finely chopped rosemary to the dough.
- Mix until a dough forms.

Knead the Dough:
- Transfer the dough to a floured surface and knead for about 8-10 minutes, or until it becomes smooth and elastic.

First Rise:
- Place the dough in a lightly oiled bowl, cover it with a clean kitchen towel, and let it rise in a warm place for about 1-2 hours, or until it doubles in size.

Shape the Bread:
- Punch down the risen dough and shape it into a round or oval loaf.

Second Rise:
- Place the shaped dough on a parchment-lined baking sheet.

- Cover with a kitchen towel and let it rise for an additional 30-45 minutes.

Preheat Oven:
- Preheat your oven to 375°F (190°C).

Prepare Topping:
- In a small bowl, mix together olive oil and chopped fresh rosemary.

Brush with Olive Oil Mixture:
- Brush the olive oil and rosemary mixture over the top of the risen bread.

Sprinkle with Sea Salt:
- Sprinkle sea salt over the top for added flavor.

Bake:
- Bake the bread in the preheated oven for 25-30 minutes, or until it's golden brown and sounds hollow when tapped.

Cool:
- Allow the Rosemary Olive Oil Bread to cool on a wire rack before slicing.

Enjoy your homemade Rosemary Olive Oil Bread! This bread is infused with the fragrant essence of rosemary and olive oil, making it a perfect accompaniment to soups, salads, or as a standalone snack.

**Zucchini Walnut Bread:**

Ingredients:

For the Bread:

- 2 cups grated zucchini (about 2 medium-sized zucchinis)
- 1/2 cup unsalted butter, melted
- 1 cup granulated sugar
- 2 large eggs
- 1 teaspoon vanilla extract
- 2 cups all-purpose flour
- 1 teaspoon baking soda
- 1/2 teaspoon baking powder
- 1/2 teaspoon salt
- 1 teaspoon ground cinnamon
- 1/2 cup chopped walnuts

For Topping (Optional):

- 2 tablespoons chopped walnuts
- 1 tablespoon granulated sugar

Directions:

Preheat Oven:
- Preheat your oven to 350°F (175°C). Grease and flour a 9x5-inch loaf pan.

Grate Zucchini:
- Grate the zucchinis using a box grater. Place the grated zucchini in a clean kitchen towel and squeeze out excess moisture.

Mix Wet Ingredients:
- In a large mixing bowl, combine the melted butter, granulated sugar, eggs, and vanilla extract. Mix until well combined.

Add Grated Zucchini:
- Stir in the grated zucchini into the wet ingredients.

Mix Dry Ingredients:
- In a separate bowl, whisk together the flour, baking soda, baking powder, salt, and ground cinnamon.

Combine Wet and Dry Ingredients:
- Gradually add the dry ingredients to the wet ingredients, mixing until just combined.

Fold in Walnuts:
- Gently fold in the chopped walnuts into the batter.

Pour into Loaf Pan:
- Pour the batter into the prepared loaf pan, spreading it evenly.

Optional Topping:
- If desired, sprinkle chopped walnuts and granulated sugar over the top of the batter.

Bake:
- Bake in the preheated oven for 55-65 minutes, or until a toothpick inserted into the center comes out clean. If the top is browning too quickly, you can loosely cover it with aluminum foil.

Cool:
- Allow the Zucchini Walnut Bread to cool in the pan for about 10 minutes, then transfer it to a wire rack to cool completely.

Slice and Serve:
- Once cooled, slice the bread into thick slices and enjoy!

This Zucchini Walnut Bread is a delightful way to use fresh zucchini and makes for a moist and flavorful treat. It's perfect for breakfast, brunch, or as a tasty snack.

**Cheesy Jalapeño Cornbread:**

Ingredients:

For the Cornbread:

- 1 cup cornmeal
- 1 cup all-purpose flour
- 1 tablespoon baking powder
- 1/2 teaspoon salt
- 1 cup buttermilk
- 1/2 cup unsalted butter, melted
- 1/4 cup honey
- 2 large eggs
- 1 cup shredded sharp cheddar cheese
- 1/4 cup pickled jalapeños, chopped

For Topping:

- 1/2 cup shredded sharp cheddar cheese
- 1 tablespoon pickled jalapeños, sliced

Directions:

Preheat Oven:
- Preheat your oven to 375°F (190°C). Grease a 9-inch square baking pan.

Mix Dry Ingredients:
- In a large mixing bowl, whisk together the cornmeal, flour, baking powder, and salt.

Combine Wet Ingredients:
- In a separate bowl, whisk together the buttermilk, melted butter, honey, and eggs.

Combine Wet and Dry Ingredients:
- Pour the wet ingredients into the dry ingredients and stir until just combined.

Fold in Cheese and Jalapeños:
- Gently fold in the shredded cheddar cheese and chopped jalapeños into the batter.

Pour into Pan:
- Pour the batter into the prepared baking pan, spreading it evenly.

Top with Cheese and Jalapeños:
- Sprinkle the top with the additional shredded cheddar cheese and sliced jalapeños.

Bake:

- Bake in the preheated oven for 25-30 minutes, or until a toothpick inserted into the center comes out clean.

Cool:
- Allow the Cheesy Jalapeño Cornbread to cool in the pan for about 10 minutes, then transfer it to a wire rack to cool completely.

Slice and Serve:
- Once cooled, cut the cornbread into squares and serve.

This Cheesy Jalapeño Cornbread is a savory and slightly spicy twist on traditional cornbread. It pairs well with chili, soups, or as a tasty side dish. Enjoy the delightful combination of cheesy goodness and a kick of jalapeño flavor!

**Cinnamon Raisin Swirl Bread:**

Ingredients:

For the Dough:

- 1 cup warm milk (110°F/43°C)
- 1/4 cup unsalted butter, melted
- 1/4 cup granulated sugar
- 2 1/4 teaspoons active dry yeast
- 3 1/2 cups all-purpose flour
- 1/2 teaspoon salt
- 1 large egg

For the Filling:

- 1/3 cup granulated sugar
- 2 teaspoons ground cinnamon
- 1 cup raisins

For the Glaze (Optional):

- 1/2 cup powdered sugar
- 1-2 tablespoons milk
- 1/2 teaspoon vanilla extract

Directions:

    Activate Yeast:
- In a small bowl, combine warm milk, melted butter, and 1 tablespoon of sugar. Stir until sugar dissolves.
- Sprinkle active dry yeast over the mixture and let it sit for 5-10 minutes until it becomes frothy.

    Prepare Dough:
- In a large mixing bowl, combine flour, remaining sugar, and salt.
- Make a well in the center and pour in the activated yeast mixture and beaten egg.
- Mix until a dough forms.

    Knead:
- Transfer the dough to a floured surface and knead for about 8-10 minutes, or until it becomes smooth and elastic.

    First Rise:

- Place the dough in a lightly oiled bowl, cover it with a clean kitchen towel, and let it rise in a warm place for about 1-2 hours, or until it doubles in size.

Prepare Filling:
- In a small bowl, mix together sugar and ground cinnamon for the filling.

Roll Out Dough:
- Punch down the risen dough and roll it out into a rectangle on a floured surface.

Add Filling and Raisins:
- Brush the surface of the dough with a bit of water.
- Sprinkle the cinnamon sugar mixture evenly over the dough.
- Scatter raisins over the cinnamon sugar.

Roll and Shape:
- Starting from one of the longer sides, tightly roll the dough into a log.
- Place the rolled dough in a greased loaf pan.

Second Rise:
- Cover the loaf pan with a kitchen towel and let it rise for an additional 30-45 minutes.

Preheat Oven:
- Preheat your oven to 350°F (175°C).

Bake:
- Bake the Cinnamon Raisin Swirl Bread in the preheated oven for 30-35 minutes, or until it's golden brown.

Cool:
- Allow the bread to cool in the pan for 10 minutes, then transfer it to a wire rack to cool completely.

Prepare Glaze (Optional):
- If desired, mix together powdered sugar, milk, and vanilla extract to create a glaze. Drizzle it over the cooled bread.

Slice and Enjoy:
- Once the glaze is set, slice and enjoy your Cinnamon Raisin Swirl Bread!

This bread is perfect for breakfast or as a sweet treat with your afternoon tea. The combination of cinnamon and raisins creates a delightful flavor that's sure to be a hit.

**Garlic and Herb Focaccia:**

Ingredients:

For the Dough:

- 3 1/2 cups all-purpose flour
- 1 1/2 cups warm water (110°F/43°C)
- 2 teaspoons active dry yeast
- 1 teaspoon sugar
- 1 teaspoon salt
- 1/4 cup olive oil

For the Topping:

- 1/4 cup olive oil
- 3 cloves garlic, minced
- 1 tablespoon fresh rosemary, chopped
- 1 tablespoon fresh thyme leaves
- Coarse sea salt for sprinkling

Directions:

Activate Yeast:
- In a small bowl, combine warm water, sugar, and active dry yeast. Let it sit for 5-10 minutes until it becomes frothy.

Prepare Dough:
- In a large mixing bowl, combine the flour and salt. Make a well in the center.
- Pour the activated yeast mixture and olive oil into the well.
- Mix until a dough forms.

Knead:
- Transfer the dough to a floured surface and knead for about 8-10 minutes, or until it becomes smooth and elastic.

First Rise:
- Place the dough in a lightly oiled bowl, cover it with a clean kitchen towel, and let it rise in a warm place for about 1-2 hours, or until it doubles in size.

Prepare Focaccia:
- Preheat your oven to 425°F (220°C).
- Punch down the risen dough and transfer it to a greased baking sheet.
- Press the dough evenly into the pan, creating dimples with your fingertips.

Prepare Topping:

- In a small bowl, mix together olive oil, minced garlic, chopped rosemary, and thyme.

Top the Dough:
- Brush the olive oil and herb mixture evenly over the surface of the focaccia.
- Sprinkle coarse sea salt over the top.

Second Rise:
- Cover the pan with a kitchen towel and let the focaccia rise for an additional 20-30 minutes.

Bake:
- Bake the Garlic and Herb Focaccia in the preheated oven for 20-25 minutes, or until it's golden brown.

Cool:
- Allow the focaccia to cool slightly before slicing.

Slice and Serve:
- Slice the focaccia into squares or wedges and serve it warm.

Enjoy your homemade Garlic and Herb Focaccia! This flavorful bread is perfect for serving as an appetizer, alongside soups, or as a delicious side dish.

**Cherry Almond Bread:**

Ingredients:

For the Bread:

- 1 cup dried cherries
- 1/2 cup hot water
- 1/2 cup unsalted butter, softened
- 1 cup granulated sugar
- 2 large eggs
- 1 teaspoon almond extract
- 2 cups all-purpose flour
- 1 teaspoon baking powder
- 1/2 teaspoon baking soda
- 1/4 teaspoon salt
- 1 cup plain Greek yogurt

For the Almond Streusel Topping:

- 1/2 cup sliced almonds
- 1/4 cup all-purpose flour
- 3 tablespoons granulated sugar
- 2 tablespoons unsalted butter, cold and cubed

For the Glaze (Optional):

- 1/2 cup powdered sugar
- 1-2 tablespoons milk
- 1/2 teaspoon almond extract

Directions:

Preheat Oven:
- Preheat your oven to 350°F (175°C). Grease and flour a 9x5-inch loaf pan.

Prepare Cherries:
- Place dried cherries in a bowl and pour hot water over them. Let them soak for 10-15 minutes, then drain.

Make Almond Streusel Topping:
- In a small bowl, combine sliced almonds, flour, sugar, and cold, cubed butter. Use your fingers to mix until crumbly. Set aside.

Prepare the Bread Batter:
- In a large mixing bowl, cream together softened butter and sugar until light and fluffy.
- Add eggs one at a time, beating well after each addition. Mix in almond extract.

Combine Dry Ingredients:
- In a separate bowl, whisk together flour, baking powder, baking soda, and salt.

Add Dry Ingredients and Yogurt:
- Gradually add the dry ingredients to the wet ingredients, alternating with the Greek yogurt. Begin and end with the dry ingredients. Mix until just combined.

Fold in Cherries:
- Gently fold in the soaked and drained cherries into the batter.

Pour into Loaf Pan:
- Pour the batter into the prepared loaf pan, spreading it evenly.

Add Almond Streusel Topping:
- Sprinkle the almond streusel topping over the batter.

Bake:
- Bake in the preheated oven for 55-65 minutes or until a toothpick inserted into the center comes out clean.

Cool:
- Allow the Cherry Almond Bread to cool in the pan for about 10 minutes, then transfer it to a wire rack to cool completely.

Prepare Glaze (Optional):
- In a small bowl, whisk together powdered sugar, milk, and almond extract to make the glaze.

Glaze the Bread:
- Once the bread has cooled, drizzle the glaze over the top.

Slice and Serve:
- Slice the Cherry Almond Bread into thick slices and enjoy!

This bread is a wonderful combination of sweet cherries, almonds, and a hint of almond extract. The streusel topping adds a delightful crunch, and the optional glaze provides an extra touch of sweetness.

**Multigrain Seeded Bread:**

Ingredients:

For the Starter (Sponge):

- 1 cup lukewarm water
- 2 teaspoons active dry yeast
- 1 cup whole wheat flour

For the Dough:

- All of the starter (sponge)
- 1 cup lukewarm milk
- 2 tablespoons honey or maple syrup
- 2 tablespoons olive oil
- 1 1/2 teaspoons salt
- 1 cup all-purpose flour (approximately)
- 1/2 cup rolled oats
- 1/4 cup flaxseeds
- 1/4 cup sunflower seeds
- 1/4 cup pumpkin seeds
- 1/4 cup sesame seeds
- 1/4 cup chia seeds

For Topping:

- Additional seeds for sprinkling on top (optional)

Directions:

**Prepare the Starter (Sponge):**

Activate Yeast:
- In a bowl, combine lukewarm water and active dry yeast. Let it sit for 5-10 minutes until frothy.

Create the Sponge:
- Add whole wheat flour to the yeast mixture, creating a thick batter.
- Cover the bowl with a cloth and let it sit in a warm place for about 30 minutes to 1 hour, allowing the sponge to ferment and become bubbly.

**Make the Dough:**

Combine Ingredients:
- In a large mixing bowl, combine the sponge, lukewarm milk, honey (or maple syrup), olive oil, and salt.

Add Grains and Seeds:
- Gradually add the all-purpose flour while stirring. Mix in the rolled oats, flaxseeds, sunflower seeds, pumpkin seeds, sesame seeds, and chia seeds.

Knead:
- Turn the dough out onto a floured surface and knead for about 10-15 minutes, or until it becomes smooth and elastic.

First Rise:
- Place the dough in a lightly oiled bowl, cover it with a clean kitchen towel, and let it rise in a warm place for about 1-2 hours, or until it doubles in size.

Shape the Loaf:
- Punch down the risen dough and shape it into a round or oval loaf.

Second Rise:
- Place the shaped dough on a parchment-lined baking sheet.
- Cover with a kitchen towel and let it rise for an additional 30-45 minutes.

Preheat Oven:
- Preheat your oven to 375°F (190°C).

Score and Seed the Bread (Optional):
- If desired, score the top of the loaf with a sharp knife and sprinkle additional seeds on top.

Bake:
- Bake the Multigrain Seeded Bread in the preheated oven for 30-35 minutes, or until it's golden brown and sounds hollow when tapped.

Cool:
- Allow the bread to cool on a wire rack before slicing.

Slice and Serve:
- Slice the Multigrain Seeded Bread into thick slices and enjoy!

This bread is not only flavorful but also loaded with the goodness of various grains and seeds. It's perfect for sandwiches, toast, or simply with a smear of butter.

**Rosemary and Olive No-Knead Bread:**

Ingredients:

For the Dough:

- 3 cups all-purpose flour
- 1 3/4 teaspoons salt
- 1/2 teaspoon active dry yeast
- 1 1/2 cups warm water (about 110°F/43°C)
- 1/2 cup pitted and chopped Kalamata olives
- 1 tablespoon fresh rosemary, finely chopped

For the Topping:

- Extra olive oil for drizzling
- Coarse sea salt for sprinkling

Directions:

Mix the Dough:
- In a large mixing bowl, combine the all-purpose flour, salt, and active dry yeast.
- Add warm water to the dry ingredients and stir until just combined. The dough will be sticky and shaggy.

Add Olives and Rosemary:
- Gently fold in the chopped Kalamata olives and fresh rosemary into the dough.

First Rise:
- Cover the bowl with plastic wrap and let the dough rise at room temperature for 12-18 hours. During this time, the dough will become bubbly and rise significantly.

Preheat Oven:
- Preheat your oven to 450°F (232°C). Place a covered Dutch oven or a heavy oven-safe pot in the oven while it preheats.

Shape the Dough:
- Generously flour a work surface and your hands. Transfer the risen dough to the floured surface, and with floured hands, shape it into a round loaf.

Second Rise:
- Place the shaped dough on parchment paper. Cover it with a clean kitchen towel and let it rise for an additional 30 minutes while the oven preheats.

Score the Dough:

- Right before baking, use a sharp knife to score the top of the dough with a few slashes.

Bake:
- Carefully remove the preheated Dutch oven from the oven. Lift the parchment paper with the dough and place it into the hot pot.
- Drizzle the top of the dough with olive oil and sprinkle coarse sea salt.

Cover and Bake:
- Cover the Dutch oven with its lid and place it back in the oven.
- Bake covered for 30 minutes.

Uncover and Bake:
- Remove the lid and continue baking for an additional 15-20 minutes or until the bread has a golden brown crust.

Cool:
- Allow the Rosemary and Olive No-Knead Bread to cool on a wire rack before slicing.

Slice and Serve:
- Slice the bread into thick slices and savor the flavors of rosemary and olives.

This no-knead bread is rustic, flavorful, and requires minimal effort. The combination of rosemary and olives adds a Mediterranean twist that makes it a great accompaniment to soups, salads, or enjoyed on its own.

Honey Whole Wheat Bread. This recipe combines the wholesome goodness of whole wheat with the sweetness of honey, resulting in a hearty and flavorful bread that's perfect for sandwiches or toast.

Ingredients:

For the Dough:

- 1 1/2 cups warm water (110°F/43°C)
- 2 tablespoons active dry yeast
- 1/4 cup honey
- 2 tablespoons olive oil
- 1 1/2 teaspoons salt
- 3 1/2 cups whole wheat flour
- 1 cup all-purpose flour (plus extra for dusting)

For Brushing (Optional):

- 1 tablespoon melted butter
- 1 tablespoon honey

Directions:

- Activate Yeast:
    - In a bowl, combine warm water, honey, and active dry yeast. Let it sit for 5-10 minutes until frothy.
- Mix Dough:
    - In a large mixing bowl, combine the activated yeast mixture, olive oil, and salt.
    - Gradually add the whole wheat flour and all-purpose flour, mixing until a dough forms.
- Knead:
    - Transfer the dough to a floured surface and knead for about 8-10 minutes, or until it becomes smooth and elastic. Add more flour if needed.
- First Rise:
    - Place the dough in a lightly oiled bowl, cover it with a clean kitchen towel, and let it rise in a warm place for about 1-2 hours, or until it doubles in size.
- Shape the Loaf:
    - Punch down the risen dough and shape it into a loaf.
- Second Rise:
    - Place the shaped dough in a greased loaf pan.
    - Cover with a kitchen towel and let it rise for an additional 30-45 minutes.
- Preheat Oven:
    - Preheat your oven to 375°F (190°C).
- Bake:
    - Bake the Honey Whole Wheat Bread in the preheated oven for 25-30 minutes, or until it's golden brown and sounds hollow when tapped.
- Brush with Butter and Honey (Optional):
    - If desired, mix melted butter and honey and brush it over the top of the bread as soon as it comes out of the oven.
- Cool:
    - Allow the bread to cool in the pan for about 10 minutes, then transfer it to a wire rack to cool completely.
- Slice and Serve:
    - Slice the Honey Whole Wheat Bread into thick slices and enjoy!

This bread is a wholesome and slightly sweet treat that's perfect for those who appreciate the nutty flavor of whole wheat and the natural sweetness of honey. It's versatile and can be enjoyed with both sweet and savory toppings.

**Sun-Dried Tomato and Basil Focaccia:**

Ingredients:

For the Dough:

- 3 1/2 cups all-purpose flour
- 1 1/2 cups warm water (110°F/43°C)
- 2 teaspoons active dry yeast
- 1 teaspoon sugar
- 1 teaspoon salt
- 1/4 cup olive oil

For the Topping:

- 1/2 cup sun-dried tomatoes (packed in oil), drained and chopped
- 2 tablespoons fresh basil, chopped
- 1/4 cup olive oil
- Coarse sea salt for sprinkling

Directions:

Activate Yeast:
- In a small bowl, combine warm water, sugar, and active dry yeast. Let it sit for 5-10 minutes until frothy.

Prepare Dough:
- In a large mixing bowl, combine the activated yeast mixture, salt, and olive oil.
- Gradually add the all-purpose flour, mixing until a dough forms.

Knead:
- Turn the dough out onto a floured surface and knead for about 10-15 minutes, or until it becomes smooth and elastic.

First Rise:
- Place the dough in a lightly oiled bowl, cover it with a clean kitchen towel, and let it rise in a warm place for about 1-2 hours, or until it doubles in size.

Prepare Focaccia:
- Preheat your oven to 425°F (218°C).
- Punch down the risen dough and transfer it to a parchment-lined baking sheet.
- Press the dough evenly into the pan, creating dimples with your fingertips.

Prepare Topping:
- In a small bowl, mix together sun-dried tomatoes, fresh basil, and olive oil.

Top the Dough:

- Spread the sun-dried tomato and basil mixture evenly over the surface of the focaccia.
- Drizzle additional olive oil over the top.
- Sprinkle coarse sea salt over the surface.

Second Rise:
- Cover the pan with a kitchen towel and let the focaccia rise for an additional 30-45 minutes.

Bake:
- Bake the Sun-Dried Tomato and Basil Focaccia in the preheated oven for 20-25 minutes, or until it's golden brown.

Cool:
- Allow the focaccia to cool slightly before slicing.

Slice and Serve:
- Slice the focaccia into squares or wedges and serve it warm.

This Sun-Dried Tomato and Basil Focaccia is a delightful bread that brings the flavors of the Mediterranean to your table. It's perfect as an appetizer, side dish, or enjoyed on its own.

**Cheese and Herb Pull-Apart Bread:**

Ingredients:

For the Dough:

- 4 cups all-purpose flour
- 2 1/4 teaspoons active dry yeast
- 1 cup warm milk (110°F/43°C)
- 1/4 cup unsalted butter, melted
- 1/4 cup granulated sugar
- 1 teaspoon salt
- 1 large egg

For the Filling:

- 1 1/2 cups shredded cheese (cheddar, mozzarella, or your favorite blend)
- 1/4 cup unsalted butter, melted
- 2 tablespoons fresh parsley, finely chopped
- 2 teaspoons dried oregano
- 1 teaspoon garlic powder

For Topping:

- Additional shredded cheese
- Fresh parsley, chopped

Directions:

Activate Yeast:
- In a small bowl, combine warm milk and active dry yeast. Let it sit for 5-10 minutes until frothy.

Prepare Dough:
- In a large mixing bowl, combine flour, sugar, and salt.
- Add the activated yeast mixture, melted butter, and egg. Mix until a dough forms.

Knead:
- Turn the dough out onto a floured surface and knead for about 8-10 minutes, or until it becomes smooth and elastic.

First Rise:

- Place the dough in a lightly oiled bowl, cover it with a clean kitchen towel, and let it rise in a warm place for about 1-2 hours, or until it doubles in size.

Prepare Filling:
- In a bowl, mix together shredded cheese, melted butter, chopped parsley, dried oregano, and garlic powder.

Shape the Bread:
- Punch down the risen dough and roll it out into a rectangle on a floured surface.
- Spread the cheese and herb filling evenly over the surface of the dough.

Cut into Strips:
- Using a sharp knife or a pizza cutter, cut the dough into strips (about 1.5 inches wide).

Stack Strips:
- Carefully stack the strips on top of each other to form a layered stack.

Cut into Squares:
- Cut the stacked strips into squares.

Second Rise:
- Place the cut squares in a greased baking dish.
- Cover with a kitchen towel and let them rise for an additional 30-45 minutes.

Preheat Oven:
- Preheat your oven to 350°F (175°C).

Bake:
- Sprinkle additional shredded cheese and chopped parsley over the top.
- Bake the Cheese and Herb Pull-Apart Bread in the preheated oven for 25-30 minutes, or until it's golden brown and the cheese is melted and bubbly.

Cool:
- Allow the bread to cool slightly before serving.

Pull Apart and Enjoy:
- Pull apart the cheesy, herby squares and enjoy this delicious and shareable bread!

This Cheese and Herb Pull-Apart Bread is perfect for gatherings or as a savory snack. The layers of cheese and herbs add a burst of flavor in every bite.

**Chocolate Swirl Babka:**

Ingredients:

For the Dough:

- 4 cups all-purpose flour
- 1/2 cup granulated sugar
- 2 1/4 teaspoons active dry yeast
- 1 cup warm milk (110°F/43°C)
- 1/2 cup unsalted butter, melted
- 2 large eggs
- 1 teaspoon vanilla extract
- 1/2 teaspoon salt

For the Chocolate Filling:

- 1 cup semisweet chocolate chips or chopped chocolate
- 1/4 cup unsalted butter
- 1/3 cup granulated sugar
- 2 tablespoons cocoa powder
- 1/2 teaspoon ground cinnamon

For the Sugar Syrup:

- 1/4 cup water
- 1/4 cup granulated sugar

Directions:

    Activate Yeast:
- In a small bowl, combine warm milk and active dry yeast. Let it sit for 5-10 minutes until frothy.

    Prepare Dough:
- In a large mixing bowl, combine flour, sugar, and salt.
- Add the activated yeast mixture, melted butter, eggs, and vanilla extract. Mix until a dough forms.

    Knead:
- Turn the dough out onto a floured surface and knead for about 8-10 minutes, or until it becomes smooth and elastic.

First Rise:
- Place the dough in a lightly oiled bowl, cover it with a clean kitchen towel, and let it rise in a warm place for about 1-2 hours, or until it doubles in size.

Prepare Chocolate Filling:
- In a saucepan over low heat, melt butter and chocolate. Stir in sugar, cocoa powder, and ground cinnamon until well combined. Remove from heat and let it cool.

Roll Out Dough:
- After the first rise, roll out the dough on a floured surface into a rectangle.

Spread Chocolate Filling:
- Spread the chocolate filling evenly over the surface of the dough.

Roll and Shape:
- Starting from one of the longer sides, tightly roll the dough into a log.

Twist the Dough:
- Cut the rolled log in half lengthwise, exposing the layers. Twist the two halves together to form a twisted loaf.

Second Rise:
- Place the twisted dough in a greased loaf pan.
- Cover with a kitchen towel and let it rise for an additional 30-45 minutes.

Preheat Oven:
- Preheat your oven to 350°F (175°C).

Bake:
- Bake the Chocolate Swirl Babka in the preheated oven for 30-35 minutes, or until it's golden brown and sounds hollow when tapped.

Prepare Sugar Syrup:
- In a small saucepan, heat water and sugar over medium heat until the sugar dissolves. Remove from heat.

Brush with Sugar Syrup:
- As soon as the babka comes out of the oven, brush the top with the sugar syrup.

Cool:
- Allow the babka to cool in the pan for 10 minutes, then transfer it to a wire rack to cool completely.

Slice and Enjoy:
- Slice the Chocolate Swirl Babka into thick slices and savor the delicious layers of chocolate and cinnamon.

This Chocolate Swirl Babka is a sweet indulgence, perfect for sharing with family and friends. Its twisted shape and rich chocolate flavor make it a showstopper for special occasions.

**Olive and Rosemary Fougasse:**

Ingredients:

For the Dough:

- 3 1/2 cups all-purpose flour
- 1 1/2 teaspoons salt
- 1 teaspoon active dry yeast
- 1 1/2 cups warm water (110°F/43°C)
- 2 tablespoons olive oil

For the Filling:

- 1 cup mixed olives (green and black), pitted and chopped
- 2 tablespoons fresh rosemary, finely chopped
- Extra olive oil for drizzling

For Topping (Optional):

- Coarse sea salt

Directions:

Activate Yeast:
- In a small bowl, combine warm water and active dry yeast. Let it sit for 5-10 minutes until frothy.

Prepare Dough:
- In a large mixing bowl, combine flour and salt.
- Add the activated yeast mixture and olive oil. Mix until a dough forms.

Knead:
- Turn the dough out onto a floured surface and knead for about 8-10 minutes, or until it becomes smooth and elastic.

First Rise:
- Place the dough in a lightly oiled bowl, cover it with a clean kitchen towel, and let it rise in a warm place for about 1-2 hours, or until it doubles in size.

Prepare Filling:
- In a bowl, mix together chopped olives and fresh rosemary.

Shape the Dough:
- After the first rise, preheat your oven to 450°F (232°C).
- Turn the dough out onto a floured surface and roll it into a rectangle.

Add Filling:
- Spread the olive and rosemary mixture evenly over the surface of the dough.

Fold and Shape:
- Fold the dough over the filling and press the edges to seal.
- Shape the dough into a leaf-like or oval shape.

Second Rise:
- Place the shaped dough on a parchment-lined baking sheet.
- Cover with a kitchen towel and let it rise for an additional 30-45 minutes.

Preheat Oven:
- Preheat your oven to 450°F (232°C).

Bake:
- If desired, drizzle extra olive oil over the top and sprinkle coarse sea salt.
- Bake the Olive and Rosemary Fougasse in the preheated oven for 20-25 minutes, or until it's golden brown and sounds hollow when tapped.

Cool:
- Allow the fougasse to cool on a wire rack before slicing.

Slice and Serve:
- Slice the Olive and Rosemary Fougasse into pieces and enjoy the wonderful combination of olives and rosemary.

This Olive and Rosemary Fougasse is a fantastic addition to a Mediterranean-themed meal or as a standalone appetizer. Its unique shape and savory filling make it a visually appealing and flavorful choice.

**Challah Bread:**

Ingredients:

For the Dough:

- 4 to 4 1/2 cups all-purpose flour
- 1/4 cup granulated sugar
- 1 packet (2 1/4 teaspoons) active dry yeast
- 1 1/4 teaspoons salt
- 1/2 cup warm water (110°F/43°C)
- 3 large eggs
- 1/4 cup vegetable oil or melted unsalted butter

For the Egg Wash:

- 1 egg, beaten
- 1 tablespoon water

Sesame seeds or poppy seeds for sprinkling (optional)

Directions:

Activate Yeast:
- In a small bowl, combine warm water, sugar, and active dry yeast. Let it sit for 5-10 minutes until frothy.

Prepare Dough:
- In a large mixing bowl, combine 4 cups of flour and salt.
- In a separate bowl, whisk together the eggs and oil. Add the activated yeast mixture.
- Pour the wet ingredients into the flour mixture and stir to form a dough.

Knead:
- Turn the dough out onto a floured surface. Knead for about 8-10 minutes, gradually adding more flour if needed, until the dough is smooth and elastic.

First Rise:
- Place the dough in a lightly oiled bowl, cover it with a clean kitchen towel, and let it rise in a warm place for about 1-2 hours, or until it doubles in size.

Shape the Dough:
- Punch down the risen dough and divide it into three equal parts.
- Roll each part into a rope, about 16 inches long.

Braid the Dough:

- Place the three ropes side by side and pinch the tops together.
- Braid the ropes, then pinch the ends together.

Second Rise:
- Place the braided dough on a parchment-lined baking sheet.
- Cover with a kitchen towel and let it rise for an additional 30-45 minutes.

Preheat Oven:
- Preheat your oven to 350°F (175°C).

Prepare Egg Wash:
- In a small bowl, beat an egg with 1 tablespoon of water.

Brush with Egg Wash:
- Brush the top of the challah with the egg wash.
- If desired, sprinkle sesame seeds or poppy seeds over the top.

Bake:
- Bake the Challah Bread in the preheated oven for 25-30 minutes, or until it's golden brown and sounds hollow when tapped.

Cool:
- Allow the challah to cool on a wire rack before slicing.

Slice and Serve:
- Slice the Challah Bread into thick slices and enjoy the soft and slightly sweet flavor.

Challah is not only delicious on its own but also makes fantastic French toast or bread pudding. Its braided appearance adds a special touch to any table.

**Multigrain Bread:**

Ingredients:

For the Sponge:

- 1 cup warm water (110°F/43°C)
- 2 teaspoons active dry yeast
- 1 cup whole wheat flour
- 1/4 cup honey or maple syrup

For the Dough:

- All of the sponge
- 1 cup warm milk (110°F/43°C)
- 1/4 cup olive oil or melted butter
- 1 1/2 teaspoons salt
- 2 cups all-purpose flour
- 1 cup whole wheat flour
- 1/2 cup rolled oats
- 1/4 cup flaxseeds
- 1/4 cup sunflower seeds
- 1/4 cup pumpkin seeds
- 1/4 cup sesame seeds
- 1/4 cup chia seeds

For the Egg Wash (Optional):

- 1 egg
- 1 tablespoon water

Directions:

Activate Yeast:
- In a small bowl, combine warm water, honey (or maple syrup), and active dry yeast. Let it sit for 5-10 minutes until frothy.

Prepare Sponge:
- In a large mixing bowl, combine the yeast mixture with 1 cup of whole wheat flour. This creates the sponge.
- Cover the bowl with a clean kitchen towel and let it sit for about 30 minutes.

Add Additional Ingredients:

- To the sponge, add warm milk, olive oil (or melted butter), and salt. Mix well.

Incorporate Grains and Seeds:
- Add all-purpose flour, additional whole wheat flour, rolled oats, flaxseeds, sunflower seeds, pumpkin seeds, sesame seeds, and chia seeds to the mixture.
- Stir until a dough forms.

Knead:
- Turn the dough out onto a floured surface and knead for about 10-12 minutes, or until it becomes smooth and elastic.

First Rise:
- Place the dough in a lightly oiled bowl, cover it with a clean kitchen towel, and let it rise in a warm place for about 1-2 hours, or until it doubles in size.

Shape the Dough:
- Punch down the risen dough and shape it into a loaf.
- Place the shaped dough in a greased loaf pan.

Second Rise:
- Cover the loaf pan with a kitchen towel and let it rise for an additional 30-45 minutes.

Preheat Oven:
- Preheat your oven to 375°F (190°C).

Prepare Egg Wash (Optional):
- In a small bowl, beat an egg with 1 tablespoon of water.

Brush with Egg Wash (Optional):
- If desired, brush the top of the bread with the egg wash for a shiny crust.

Bake:
- Bake the Multigrain Bread in the preheated oven for 35-40 minutes, or until it's golden brown and sounds hollow when tapped.

Cool:
- Allow the bread to cool in the pan for 10 minutes, then transfer it to a wire rack to cool completely.

Slice and Enjoy:
- Slice the Multigrain Bread into thick slices and savor the nutty flavor and hearty texture.

This Multigrain Bread is not only delicious but also nutritious with the addition of various grains and seeds. It's a versatile option that can be enjoyed in a variety of ways.

**Cranberry Walnut Bread:**

Ingredients:

For the Dough:

- 3 1/2 cups all-purpose flour
- 1 1/2 teaspoons salt
- 2 teaspoons active dry yeast
- 1 1/2 cups warm water (110°F/43°C)
- 1/4 cup honey or maple syrup
- 1/4 cup olive oil or melted butter

For the Filling:

- 1 cup dried cranberries
- 1 cup chopped walnuts

For the Egg Wash (Optional):

- 1 egg
- 1 tablespoon water

Directions:

  Activate Yeast:
  - In a small bowl, combine warm water, honey (or maple syrup), and active dry yeast. Let it sit for 5-10 minutes until frothy.
  
  Prepare Dough:
  - In a large mixing bowl, combine flour and salt.
  - Add the activated yeast mixture and olive oil (or melted butter). Mix until a dough forms.
  
  Knead:
  - Turn the dough out onto a floured surface and knead for about 8-10 minutes, or until it becomes smooth and elastic.
  
  First Rise:
  - Place the dough in a lightly oiled bowl, cover it with a clean kitchen towel, and let it rise in a warm place for about 1-2 hours, or until it doubles in size.
  
  Add Cranberries and Walnuts:
  - Punch down the risen dough and turn it out onto a floured surface.
  - Spread dried cranberries and chopped walnuts over the dough.

Fold and Shape:
- Fold the dough over the filling and knead lightly to distribute the cranberries and walnuts evenly.

Shape the Dough:
- Shape the dough into a loaf and place it in a greased loaf pan.

Second Rise:
- Cover the loaf pan with a kitchen towel and let it rise for an additional 30-45 minutes.

Preheat Oven:
- Preheat your oven to 375°F (190°C).

Prepare Egg Wash (Optional):
- In a small bowl, beat an egg with 1 tablespoon of water.

Brush with Egg Wash (Optional):
- If desired, brush the top of the bread with the egg wash for a shiny crust.

Bake:
- Bake the Cranberry Walnut Bread in the preheated oven for 35-40 minutes, or until it's golden brown and sounds hollow when tapped.

Cool:
- Allow the bread to cool in the pan for 10 minutes, then transfer it to a wire rack to cool completely.

Slice and Enjoy:
- Slice the Cranberry Walnut Bread into thick slices and enjoy the delightful combination of cranberries and walnuts.

This Cranberry Walnut Bread is a wonderful blend of sweetness and nuttiness, making it a delightful choice for any occasion.

**Sun-Dried Tomato and Basil Bread:**

Ingredients:

For the Dough:

- 4 cups all-purpose flour
- 1 1/2 teaspoons salt
- 2 teaspoons active dry yeast
- 1 1/2 cups warm water (110°F/43°C)
- 1/4 cup olive oil
- 1/4 cup chopped sun-dried tomatoes (packed in oil, drained)
- 2 tablespoons fresh basil, chopped (or 2 teaspoons dried basil)

For the Topping:

- 2 tablespoons chopped sun-dried tomatoes
- 1 tablespoon fresh basil, chopped (or 1 teaspoon dried basil)
- Olive oil for brushing

Directions:

Activate Yeast:
- In a small bowl, combine warm water and active dry yeast. Let it sit for 5-10 minutes until frothy.

Prepare Dough:
- In a large mixing bowl, combine flour and salt.
- Add the activated yeast mixture, olive oil, chopped sun-dried tomatoes, and fresh basil. Mix until a dough forms.

Knead:
- Turn the dough out onto a floured surface and knead for about 8-10 minutes, or until it becomes smooth and elastic.

First Rise:
- Place the dough in a lightly oiled bowl, cover it with a clean kitchen towel, and let it rise in a warm place for about 1-2 hours, or until it doubles in size.

Add Topping Ingredients:
- Punch down the risen dough and turn it out onto a floured surface.
- Spread chopped sun-dried tomatoes and fresh basil over the dough.

Fold and Shape:

- Fold the dough over the topping ingredients and knead lightly to distribute them evenly.

Shape the Dough:
- Shape the dough into a round or oval loaf and place it on a parchment-lined baking sheet.

Second Rise:
- Cover the loaf with a kitchen towel and let it rise for an additional 30-45 minutes.

Preheat Oven:
- Preheat your oven to 375°F (190°C).

Brush with Olive Oil:
- Brush the top of the bread with olive oil.

Bake:
- Bake the Sun-Dried Tomato and Basil Bread in the preheated oven for 35-40 minutes, or until it's golden brown and sounds hollow when tapped.

Cool:
- Allow the bread to cool on a wire rack before slicing.

Slice and Enjoy:
- Slice the Sun-Dried Tomato and Basil Bread into thick slices and savor the wonderful combination of flavors.

This Sun-Dried Tomato and Basil Bread is a savory delight that brings the taste of the Mediterranean to your table. It's a great choice for those who enjoy bold and aromatic flavors in their bread.

**Cheese and Herb Filled Pull-Apart Bread:**

Ingredients:

For the Dough:

- 4 cups all-purpose flour
- 1/4 cup granulated sugar
- 2 1/4 teaspoons active dry yeast
- 1 teaspoon salt
- 1 cup warm milk (110°F/43°C)
- 1/4 cup unsalted butter, melted
- 2 large eggs

For the Filling:

- 1 1/2 cups shredded mozzarella cheese
- 1/2 cup grated Parmesan cheese
- 1/4 cup unsalted butter, softened
- 2 tablespoons fresh parsley, finely chopped
- 1 tablespoon fresh basil, finely chopped
- 1 tablespoon fresh chives, finely chopped
- 1 teaspoon garlic powder
- Salt and pepper to taste

For the Topping:

- 2 tablespoons unsalted butter, melted
- 1 tablespoon fresh parsley, finely chopped
- 1 tablespoon grated Parmesan cheese

Directions:

Activate Yeast:
- In a small bowl, combine warm milk and active dry yeast. Let it sit for 5-10 minutes until frothy.

Prepare Dough:
- In a large mixing bowl, combine flour, sugar, and salt.
- Add the activated yeast mixture, melted butter, and eggs. Mix until a dough forms.

Knead:

- Turn the dough out onto a floured surface and knead for about 8-10 minutes, or until it becomes smooth and elastic.

First Rise:
- Place the dough in a lightly oiled bowl, cover it with a clean kitchen towel, and let it rise in a warm place for about 1-2 hours, or until it doubles in size.

Prepare Filling:
- In a bowl, mix together shredded mozzarella, grated Parmesan, softened butter, chopped parsley, chopped basil, chopped chives, garlic powder, salt, and pepper.

Roll Out Dough:
- After the first rise, roll out the dough on a floured surface into a large rectangle.

Spread Filling:
- Spread the cheese and herb filling evenly over the surface of the dough.

Shape and Cut:
- Cut the dough into smaller squares or rectangles.
- Stack the squares with the filling facing up to create layers.

Place in Pan:
- Place the stacked squares in a greased loaf pan.

Second Rise:
- Cover the loaf pan with a kitchen towel and let it rise for an additional 30-45 minutes.

Preheat Oven:
- Preheat your oven to 350°F (175°C).

Prepare Topping:
- In a small bowl, mix together melted butter, chopped parsley, and grated Parmesan.

Brush with Topping:
- Brush the top of the pull-apart bread with the buttery topping.

Bake:
- Bake the Cheese and Herb Filled Pull-Apart Bread in the preheated oven for 30-35 minutes, or until it's golden brown and sounds hollow when tapped.

Cool:
- Allow the bread to cool in the pan for 10 minutes, then transfer it to a wire rack to cool completely.

Pull Apart and Enjoy:
- Serve the Cheese and Herb Filled Pull-Apart Bread warm. Pull apart the layers and savor the cheesy, herby goodness.

This Cheese and Herb Filled Pull-Apart Bread is a delightful and crowd-pleasing choice for any gathering.

**Caramelized Onion and Gruyère Swirl Bread:**

Ingredients:

*For the Dough:*

- 4 cups all-purpose flour
- 1/4 cup granulated sugar
- 2 1/4 teaspoons active dry yeast
- 1 teaspoon salt
- 1 cup warm milk (110°F/43°C)
- 1/4 cup unsalted butter, melted
- 2 large eggs

*For the Filling:*

- 2 large onions, thinly sliced
- 1/4 cup unsalted butter
- 1 1/2 cups shredded Gruyère cheese
- 1/2 cup grated Parmesan cheese
- 2 tablespoons fresh thyme, finely chopped
- 1 tablespoon fresh rosemary, finely chopped
- Salt and pepper to taste

*For the Topping:*

- 2 tablespoons unsalted butter, melted
- 1 tablespoon fresh thyme, finely chopped
- 1 tablespoon grated Parmesan cheese

Directions:

Caramelize Onions:

In a pan over medium heat, melt 1/4 cup of butter. Add thinly sliced onions and cook, stirring occasionally, until they are golden brown and caramelized. Set aside to cool.

Activate Yeast:

2. In a small bowl, combine warm milk and active dry yeast. Let it sit for 5-10 minutes until frothy.

Prepare Dough:

3. In a large mixing bowl, combine flour, sugar, and salt. Add the activated yeast mixture, melted butter, and eggs. Mix until a dough forms.

Knead:

4. Turn the dough out onto a floured surface and knead for about 8-10 minutes, or until it becomes smooth and elastic.

First Rise:

5. Place the dough in a lightly oiled bowl, cover it with a clean kitchen towel, and let it rise in a warm place for about 1-2 hours, or until it doubles in size.

Prepare Filling:

6. In a bowl, mix together shredded Gruyère, grated Parmesan, caramelized onions, chopped thyme, chopped rosemary, salt, and pepper.

Roll Out Dough:

7. After the first rise, roll out the dough on a floured surface into a large rectangle.

Spread Filling:

8. Spread the Gruyère and caramelized onion filling evenly over the surface of the dough.

Shape and Cut:

9. Cut the dough into smaller squares or rectangles. Stack the squares with the filling facing up to create layers.

Place in Pan:

10. Place the stacked squares in a greased loaf pan.

Second Rise:

11. Cover the loaf pan with a kitchen towel and let it rise for an additional 30-45 minutes.

Preheat Oven:

12. Preheat your oven to 350°F (175°C).

Prepare Topping:

13. In a small bowl, mix together melted butter, chopped thyme, and grated Parmesan.

Brush with Topping:

14. Brush the top of the swirl bread with the buttery topping.

Bake:

15. Bake the Caramelized Onion and Gruyère Swirl Bread in the preheated oven for 30-35 minutes, or until it's golden brown and sounds hollow when tapped.

Cool:

16. Allow the bread to cool in the pan for 10 minutes, then transfer it to a wire rack to cool completely.

Pull Apart and Enjoy:

17. Serve the Caramelized Onion and Gruyère Swirl Bread warm. Pull apart the layers and relish the rich, savory flavors.

This delightful and flavorful swirl bread is sure to be a hit at any gathering, offering a perfect balance of sweet caramelized onions and the nutty goodness of Gruyère cheese.

**Honey Walnut Whole Wheat Bread:**

Ingredients:

*For the Dough:*

- 3 cups whole wheat flour
- 1 cup all-purpose flour
- 2 1/4 teaspoons active dry yeast
- 1 1/2 teaspoons salt
- 1 1/4 cups warm water (110°F/43°C)
- 1/4 cup honey
- 1/4 cup unsalted butter, softened

*For the Filling:*

- 1 cup chopped walnuts
- 1/4 cup honey
- 1/4 cup unsalted butter, melted
- 1 teaspoon ground cinnamon
- A pinch of salt

*For the Topping:*

- 2 tablespoons honey
- 1/4 cup chopped walnuts

Directions:

Activate Yeast:

In a small bowl, combine warm water, honey, and active dry yeast. Let it sit for 5-10 minutes until frothy.

Prepare Dough:

2. In a large mixing bowl, combine whole wheat flour, all-purpose flour, salt, and softened butter. Add the activated yeast mixture and mix until a dough forms.

Knead:

3. Turn the dough out onto a floured surface and knead for about 8-10 minutes, or until it becomes smooth and elastic.

First Rise:

4. Place the dough in a lightly oiled bowl, cover it with a clean kitchen towel, and let it rise in a warm place for about 1-2 hours, or until it doubles in size.

Prepare Filling:

5. In a bowl, mix together chopped walnuts, honey, melted butter, ground cinnamon, and a pinch of salt.

Roll Out Dough:

6. After the first rise, roll out the dough on a floured surface into a rectangle.

Spread Filling:

7. Spread the honey walnut filling evenly over the surface of the dough.

Shape and Roll:

8. Roll up the dough tightly, sealing the edges. Place the rolled dough in a greased loaf pan.

Second Rise:

9. Cover the loaf pan with a kitchen towel and let it rise for an additional 30-45 minutes.

Preheat Oven:

10. Preheat your oven to 350°F (175°C).

Bake:

11. Bake the Honey Walnut Whole Wheat Bread in the preheated oven for 35-40 minutes, or until it's golden brown and sounds hollow when tapped.

Cool:

12. Allow the bread to cool in the pan for 10 minutes, then transfer it to a wire rack.

Drizzle with Honey:

13. While the bread is still warm, drizzle honey over the top.

Sprinkle with Walnuts:

14. Sprinkle chopped walnuts on top for added texture and visual appeal.

Slice and Enjoy:

15. Slice the bread and savor the delightful combination of whole wheat goodness, honey sweetness, and crunchy walnuts.

This Honey Walnut Whole Wheat Bread is a wholesome and nutty treat, perfect for breakfast or as a delicious accompaniment to your favorite spreads. The natural sweetness of honey and the rich flavor of walnuts make this bread a delightful choice for any occasion.

**Rosemary Olive No-Knead Bread:**

Ingredients:

*For the Dough:*

- 3 cups all-purpose flour
- 1 1/2 teaspoons salt
- 1/4 teaspoon active dry yeast
- 1 1/2 cups warm water (110°F/43°C)

*For the Filling:*

- 1 cup Kalamata olives, pitted and chopped
- 2 tablespoons fresh rosemary, finely chopped
- 1/4 cup extra-virgin olive oil

*For the Topping:*

- Coarse sea salt
- Fresh rosemary leaves

Directions:

Prepare Dough:

In a large mixing bowl, combine all-purpose flour, salt, and active dry yeast. Add warm water and mix until a sticky dough forms. Cover the bowl with plastic wrap and let it rest at room temperature for 12-18 hours.

Preheat Oven:

2. Preheat your oven to 450°F (232°C). Place a covered Dutch oven or a heavy oven-safe pot in the oven to heat.

Prepare Filling:

3. In a bowl, mix together chopped Kalamata olives, chopped rosemary, and extra-virgin olive oil.

Fold in Filling:

4. After the initial rise, gently fold the olive and rosemary mixture into the dough, incorporating it evenly.

Second Rise:

5. Cover the bowl again and let the dough rise for an additional 1-2 hours until doubled in size.

Shape and Rest:

6. Turn the dough out onto a well-floured surface. Shape it into a round loaf and let it rest on parchment paper for about 30 minutes.

Score and Season:

7. Score the top of the loaf with a sharp knife. Sprinkle coarse sea salt and fresh rosemary leaves on the surface.

Bake:

8. Carefully transfer the parchment paper with the shaped dough into the preheated Dutch oven or pot. Cover and bake for 30 minutes. Then, uncover and bake for an additional 10-15 minutes or until the bread is golden brown.

Cool:

9. Allow the Rosemary Olive No-Knead Bread to cool on a wire rack for at least 1 hour before slicing.

Slice and Serve:

10. Slice the bread and enjoy the rustic, flavorful combination of rosemary-infused dough and the briny goodness of Kalamata olives.

This easy-to-make Rosemary Olive No-Knead Bread is perfect for those who love the robust flavors of rosemary and olives. With a crispy crust and a soft, chewy interior, it's a delightful artisan-style bread that pairs well with dips, spreads, or simply a drizzle of olive oil.

**Cheddar and Jalapeño Artisan Sourdough:**

Ingredients:

*For the Sourdough Starter:*

- 1 cup all-purpose flour
- 1/2 cup lukewarm water
- 1/4 cup active sourdough starter

*For the Dough:*

- 2 cups bread flour
- 1 cup all-purpose flour
- 1 1/2 teaspoons salt
- 1 1/4 cups lukewarm water
- 1 cup shredded sharp cheddar cheese
- 2-3 jalapeños, finely chopped (adjust to taste)

*For Topping:*

- 1/4 cup shredded sharp cheddar cheese
- Sliced jalapeños for garnish

Directions:

Prepare Sourdough Starter:

In a bowl, combine all-purpose flour, lukewarm water, and active sourdough starter. Mix well, cover loosely, and let it ferment at room temperature for at least 8 hours or overnight.

Mix Dough:

2. In a large bowl, combine bread flour, all-purpose flour, and salt. Add the sourdough starter mixture and lukewarm water. Mix until a shaggy dough forms.

Autolyse:

3. Cover the bowl and let the dough rest for 30 minutes. This is called the autolyse phase.

Incorporate Cheese and Jalapeños:

4. Fold in shredded cheddar cheese and finely chopped jalapeños into the dough, ensuring even distribution.

Bulk Fermentation:

5. Cover the bowl and let the dough undergo bulk fermentation for 3-4 hours, folding every 30 minutes during the first 2 hours.

Shape and Final Rise:

6. Shape the dough into a round loaf and place it in a well-floured proofing basket. Allow it to undergo a final rise for 1-2 hours or until visibly puffy.

Preheat Oven:

7. Preheat your oven to 450°F (232°C). Place a Dutch oven with a lid inside to heat.

Score and Bake:

8. Score the top of the dough with a sharp knife. Carefully transfer the dough into the preheated Dutch oven. Sprinkle additional shredded cheddar on top and garnish with sliced jalapeños. Cover and bake for 20 minutes, then uncover and bake for an additional 20-25 minutes or until the bread is golden brown and sounds hollow when tapped.

Cool:

9. Allow the Cheddar and Jalapeño Artisan Sourdough to cool on a wire rack for at least 1 hour before slicing.

Slice and Enjoy:

10. Slice the bread and relish the tangy notes of sourdough, combined with the sharpness of cheddar and a hint of jalapeño spice.

This Cheddar and Jalapeño Artisan Sourdough brings a perfect blend of cheesy goodness and a subtle kick of heat. The crusty exterior and soft, flavorful interior make it a fantastic choice for those who appreciate a bit of boldness in their bread.

**Honey Oat Whole Grain Bread:**

Ingredients:

*For the Dough:*

- 3 cups whole wheat flour
- 1 cup all-purpose flour
- 1/2 cup rolled oats
- 2 1/4 teaspoons active dry yeast
- 1 1/2 teaspoons salt
- 1 1/4 cups warm water (110°F/43°C)
- 1/4 cup honey
- 1/4 cup unsalted butter, melted

*For the Topping:*

- 2 tablespoons rolled oats
- 1 tablespoon honey

Directions:

Activate Yeast:

In a small bowl, combine warm water, honey, and active dry yeast. Let it sit for 5-10 minutes until frothy.

Prepare Dough:

2. In a large mixing bowl, combine whole wheat flour, all-purpose flour, rolled oats, and salt. Add the activated yeast mixture and melted butter. Mix until a dough forms.

Knead:

3. Turn the dough out onto a floured surface and knead for about 8-10 minutes, or until it becomes smooth and elastic.

First Rise:

4. Place the dough in a lightly oiled bowl, cover it with a clean kitchen towel, and let it rise in a warm place for about 1-2 hours, or until it doubles in size.

Shape and Second Rise:

5. Punch down the dough and shape it into a loaf. Place it in a greased loaf pan. Cover the pan with a kitchen towel and let it rise for an additional 30-45 minutes.

Preheat Oven:

6. Preheat your oven to 350°F (175°C).

Brush with Honey and Sprinkle Oats:

7. Brush the top of the loaf with honey and sprinkle rolled oats for a sweet and textured finish.

Bake:

8. Bake the Honey Oat Whole Grain Bread in the preheated oven for 30-35 minutes, or until it's golden brown and sounds hollow when tapped.

Cool:

9. Allow the bread to cool in the pan for 10 minutes, then transfer it to a wire rack.

Slice and Enjoy:

10. Slice the bread and savor the wholesome combination of whole wheat, honey, and oats. It's perfect for sandwiches, toasting, or simply with a smear of butter.

This Honey Oat Whole Grain Bread offers a nutritious and slightly sweet option for those who appreciate the heartiness of whole grains. The addition of honey and oats provides a delightful flavor and texture, making it a versatile choice for various meals.

**Sunflower Seed and Flaxseed Multigrain Bread:**

Ingredients:

*For the Dough:*

- 2 cups whole wheat flour
- 1 cup bread flour
- 1/2 cup rolled oats
- 2 tablespoons ground flaxseeds
- 2 tablespoons sunflower seeds
- 2 1/4 teaspoons active dry yeast
- 1 1/2 teaspoons salt
- 1 1/4 cups warm water (110°F/43°C)
- 2 tablespoons honey
- 2 tablespoons olive oil

*For the Topping:*

- 2 tablespoons sunflower seeds
- 1 tablespoon rolled oats

Directions:

Activate Yeast:

In a small bowl, combine warm water, honey, and active dry yeast. Let it sit for 5-10 minutes until frothy.

Prepare Dough:

2. In a large mixing bowl, combine whole wheat flour, bread flour, rolled oats, ground flaxseeds, sunflower seeds, and salt. Add the activated yeast mixture and olive oil. Mix until a dough forms.

Knead:

3. Turn the dough out onto a floured surface and knead for about 8-10 minutes, or until it becomes smooth and elastic.

First Rise:

4. Place the dough in a lightly oiled bowl, cover it with a clean kitchen towel, and let it rise in a warm place for about 1-2 hours, or until it doubles in size.

Shape and Second Rise:

5. Punch down the dough and shape it into a round or oval loaf. Place it on a parchment-lined baking sheet. Cover with a kitchen towel and let it rise for an additional 30-45 minutes.

Preheat Oven:

6. Preheat your oven to 375°F (190°C).

Brush with Water and Sprinkle Seeds:

7. Brush the top of the loaf with water and sprinkle sunflower seeds and rolled oats for a nutty and textured crust.

Bake:

8. Bake the Sunflower Seed and Flaxseed Multigrain Bread in the preheated oven for 35-40 minutes, or until it's golden brown and sounds hollow when tapped.

Cool:

9. Allow the bread to cool on a wire rack for at least 1 hour before slicing.

Slice and Enjoy:

10. Slice the bread and relish the hearty goodness of whole wheat, the crunch of sunflower seeds, and the nutritional benefits of flaxseeds. Perfect for sandwiches, toasts, or alongside your favorite soups.

This Sunflower Seed and Flaxseed Multigrain Bread is a wholesome and nutritious choice, packed with the goodness of seeds and whole grains. Its nutty flavor and hearty texture make it a great addition to your daily bread repertoire.

**Garlic and Rosemary Fougasse:**

Ingredients:

*For the Dough:*

- 3 cups bread flour
- 1 1/2 teaspoons salt
- 2 1/4 teaspoons active dry yeast
- 1 1/4 cups lukewarm water (110°F/43°C)
- 2 tablespoons olive oil

*For the Garlic and Rosemary Infusion:*

- 1/4 cup olive oil
- 4 cloves garlic, minced
- 1 tablespoon fresh rosemary, finely chopped
- Salt and black pepper to taste

Directions:

Activate Yeast:

In a small bowl, combine lukewarm water and active dry yeast. Let it sit for 5-10 minutes until frothy.

Prepare Dough:

2. In a large mixing bowl, combine bread flour and salt. Add the activated yeast mixture and olive oil. Mix until a dough forms.

Knead:

3. Turn the dough out onto a floured surface and knead for about 8-10 minutes, or until it becomes smooth and elastic.

First Rise:

4. Place the dough in a lightly oiled bowl, cover it with a clean kitchen towel, and let it rise in a warm place for about 1-2 hours, or until it doubles in size.

Prepare Infusion:

5. In a small pan, heat 1/4 cup olive oil over medium heat. Add minced garlic and chopped rosemary. Cook for 1-2 minutes until fragrant. Season with salt and black pepper. Set aside to cool.

Shape Fougasse:

6. Preheat your oven to 425°F (218°C). Line a baking sheet with parchment paper.

> Roll out the risen dough into a large oval or rectangular shape on the prepared baking sheet.
> Use a sharp knife to make several long, irregular slashes in the dough, creating a leaf-like pattern. Gently pull apart the dough at the slashes to create openings.

Garlic and Rosemary Infusion:

9. Brush the garlic and rosemary-infused oil over the top and into the openings of the fougasse.

Second Rise:

10. Cover the fougasse with a kitchen towel and let it rise for an additional 30-45 minutes.

Bake:

11. Bake the Garlic and Rosemary Fougasse in the preheated oven for 20-25 minutes, or until it's golden brown and sounds hollow when tapped.

Cool:

12. Allow the fougasse to cool on the baking sheet for 10 minutes, then transfer it to a wire rack.

Slice and Enjoy:

13. Slice the bread and savor the aromatic combination of garlic and rosemary. This fougasse is a wonderful accompaniment to soups, salads, or enjoyed on its own.

This Garlic and Rosemary Fougasse is a visually stunning and flavorful bread, perfect for sharing. The unique shape and infusion of garlic and rosemary create a deliciously fragrant and savory experience.

**Maple Pecan Whole Wheat Bread:**

Ingredients:

*For the Dough:*

- 2 1/2 cups whole wheat flour
- 1 cup bread flour
- 1/2 cup chopped pecans
- 2 1/4 teaspoons active dry yeast
- 1 1/2 teaspoons salt
- 1 cup lukewarm water (110°F/43°C)
- 1/4 cup pure maple syrup
- 2 tablespoons unsalted butter, melted

*For the Filling:*

- 1/4 cup pure maple syrup
- 1/2 cup chopped pecans
- 1 teaspoon ground cinnamon

Directions:

Activate Yeast:

In a small bowl, combine lukewarm water, maple syrup, and active dry yeast. Let it sit for 5-10 minutes until frothy.

Prepare Dough:

2. In a large mixing bowl, combine whole wheat flour, bread flour, chopped pecans, and salt. Add the activated yeast mixture and melted butter. Mix until a dough forms.

Knead:

3. Turn the dough out onto a floured surface and knead for about 8-10 minutes, or until it becomes smooth and elastic.

First Rise:

4. Place the dough in a lightly oiled bowl, cover it with a clean kitchen towel, and let it rise in a warm place for about 1-2 hours, or until it doubles in size.

Prepare Filling:

5. In a bowl, mix together chopped pecans, maple syrup, and ground cinnamon.

Shape and Fill:

6. Punch down the risen dough and roll it out into a rectangle. Spread the pecan and maple syrup filling evenly over the surface of the dough.

Roll up the dough tightly, sealing the edges. Place the rolled dough in a greased loaf pan.

Second Rise:

8. Cover the loaf pan with a kitchen towel and let it rise for an additional 30-45 minutes.

Preheat Oven:

9. Preheat your oven to 350°F (175°C).

Bake:

10. Bake the Maple Pecan Whole Wheat Bread in the preheated oven for 30-35 minutes, or until it's golden brown and sounds hollow when tapped.

Cool:

11. Allow the bread to cool in the pan for 10 minutes, then transfer it to a wire rack.

Slice and Enjoy:

12. Slice the bread and enjoy the delightful combination of whole wheat, rich maple syrup, and the crunch of pecans. This bread is perfect for breakfast or as a sweet addition to your bread basket.

This Maple Pecan Whole Wheat Bread is a sweet and nutty treat, combining the warmth of maple syrup with the richness of pecans. It's a deliciously comforting bread that brings a touch of sweetness to your table.

**Herb and Onion Focaccia:**

Ingredients:

*For the Dough:*

- 3 cups all-purpose flour
- 1 1/2 teaspoons salt
- 2 1/4 teaspoons active dry yeast
- 1 1/4 cups lukewarm water (110°F/43°C)
- 2 tablespoons olive oil

*For the Topping:*

- 1/4 cup olive oil
- 1 large red onion, thinly sliced
- 2 tablespoons fresh rosemary, chopped
- 1 tablespoon fresh thyme, chopped
- 1 teaspoon garlic powder
- Salt and black pepper to taste
- Coarse sea salt for sprinkling

Directions:

Activate Yeast:

In a small bowl, combine lukewarm water and active dry yeast. Let it sit for 5-10 minutes until frothy.

Prepare Dough:

2. In a large mixing bowl, combine all-purpose flour and salt. Add the activated yeast mixture and olive oil. Mix until a dough forms.

Knead:

3. Turn the dough out onto a floured surface and knead for about 8-10 minutes, or until it becomes smooth and elastic.

First Rise:

4. Place the dough in a lightly oiled bowl, cover it with a clean kitchen towel, and let it rise in a warm place for about 1-2 hours, or until it doubles in size.

Prepare Topping:

5. In a pan, heat 1/4 cup olive oil over medium heat. Add sliced red onions and sauté until caramelized. Add fresh rosemary, thyme, garlic powder, salt, and black pepper. Cook for an additional 2-3 minutes. Set aside.

Shape Focaccia:

6. Preheat your oven to 425°F (218°C). Grease a baking sheet or line it with parchment paper.

> Roll out the risen dough on the prepared baking sheet, shaping it into a rectangle or oval. Use your fingers to create dimples on the surface of the dough.

Add Topping:

9. Spread the onion and herb mixture evenly over the dough, making sure to get the mixture into the dimples.

Second Rise:

10. Cover the focaccia with a kitchen towel and let it rise for an additional 30-45 minutes.

Bake:

11. Sprinkle coarse sea salt over the top. Bake the Herb and Onion Focaccia in the preheated oven for 20-25 minutes, or until it's golden brown.

Cool:

12. Allow the focaccia to cool on the baking sheet for 10 minutes, then transfer it to a wire rack.

Slice and Enjoy:

13. Slice the focaccia into squares or rectangles. Serve it warm as a delightful side or appetizer.

This Herb and Onion Focaccia is a savory and aromatic bread that's perfect for sharing. The combination of caramelized onions and fresh herbs creates a flavorful topping that complements the soft and pillowy texture of the focaccia.

**Sundried Tomato and Basil Focaccia:**

Ingredients:

*For the Dough:*

- 3 cups bread flour
- 1 1/2 teaspoons salt
- 2 1/4 teaspoons active dry yeast
- 1 1/4 cups lukewarm water (110°F/43°C)
- 2 tablespoons olive oil

*For the Topping:*

- 1/4 cup olive oil
- 1/2 cup sundried tomatoes, chopped
- 1/4 cup fresh basil, chopped
- 2 cloves garlic, minced
- 1 teaspoon dried oregano
- Salt and black pepper to taste
- Grated Parmesan cheese for finishing

Directions:

Activate Yeast:

In a small bowl, combine lukewarm water and active dry yeast. Let it sit for 5-10 minutes until frothy.

Prepare Dough:

2. In a large mixing bowl, combine bread flour and salt. Add the activated yeast mixture and olive oil. Mix until a dough forms.

Knead:

3. Turn the dough out onto a floured surface and knead for about 8-10 minutes, or until it becomes smooth and elastic.

First Rise:

4. Place the dough in a lightly oiled bowl, cover it with a clean kitchen towel, and let it rise in a warm place for about 1-2 hours, or until it doubles in size.

Prepare Topping:

5. In a bowl, mix together olive oil, sundried tomatoes, fresh basil, minced garlic, dried oregano, salt, and black pepper.

Shape Focaccia:

6. Preheat your oven to 425°F (218°C). Grease a baking sheet or line it with parchment paper.

> Roll out the risen dough on the prepared baking sheet, shaping it into a rectangle or oval. Use your fingers to create dimples on the surface of the dough.

Add Topping:

9. Spread the sundried tomato and basil mixture evenly over the dough, making sure to get the mixture into the dimples.

Second Rise:

10. Cover the focaccia with a kitchen towel and let it rise for an additional 30-45 minutes.

Bake:

11. Bake the Sundried Tomato and Basil Focaccia in the preheated oven for 20-25 minutes, or until it's golden brown.

Finish with Parmesan:

12. Sprinkle grated Parmesan cheese over the top during the last 5 minutes of baking for a savory finish.

Cool:

13. Allow the focaccia to cool on the baking sheet for 10 minutes, then transfer it to a wire rack.

Slice and Enjoy:

14. Slice the focaccia into squares or rectangles. Serve it warm as a flavorful accompaniment to meals or enjoy it on its own.

This Sundried Tomato and Basil Focaccia is a burst of Mediterranean flavors with the sweetness of sundried tomatoes, the freshness of basil, and the savory notes of garlic and Parmesan. It's a versatile bread that adds a touch of sophistication to your table.

**Olive and Herb Ciabatta:**

Ingredients:

*For the Dough:*

- 3 cups bread flour
- 1 1/2 teaspoons salt
- 2 1/4 teaspoons active dry yeast
- 1 1/4 cups lukewarm water (110°F/43°C)
- 2 tablespoons olive oil

*For the Olive and Herb Mix:*

- 1/2 cup Kalamata olives, pitted and chopped
- 1/4 cup green olives, pitted and chopped
- 2 tablespoons fresh rosemary, finely chopped
- 1 tablespoon fresh thyme, finely chopped
- 2 cloves garlic, minced
- 2 tablespoons olive oil
- Salt and black pepper to taste

Directions:

Activate Yeast:

In a small bowl, combine lukewarm water and active dry yeast. Let it sit for 5-10 minutes until frothy.

Prepare Dough:

2. In a large mixing bowl, combine bread flour and salt. Add the activated yeast mixture and olive oil. Mix until a sticky dough forms.

Knead:

3. Turn the dough out onto a generously floured surface and knead for about 8-10 minutes, or until it becomes smooth and elastic. The dough will remain slightly sticky.

First Rise:

4. Place the dough in a lightly oiled bowl, cover it with a clean kitchen towel, and let it rise in a warm place for about 1-2 hours, or until it doubles in size.

Prepare Olive and Herb Mix:

5. In a bowl, mix together Kalamata olives, green olives, fresh rosemary, fresh thyme, minced garlic, olive oil, salt, and black pepper.

Fold in Olive and Herb Mix:

6. Gently fold the olive and herb mix into the risen dough, incorporating it evenly.

Second Rise:

7. Cover the bowl with the dough and olive mix and let it rise for an additional 30-45 minutes.

Preheat Oven:

8. Preheat your oven to 450°F (232°C). Place a baking stone or inverted baking sheet inside to heat.

Shape Ciabatta:

9. Turn the dough out onto a floured surface. Divide it into two portions and shape each into a rustic oval.

Bake:

10. Carefully transfer the shaped ciabatta onto the preheated baking stone or sheet. Bake for 20-25 minutes, or until the bread is golden brown and has a crispy crust.

Cool:

11. Allow the Olive and Herb Ciabatta to cool on a wire rack for at least 30 minutes before slicing.

Slice and Enjoy:

12. Slice the ciabatta and savor the aromatic blend of olives, herbs, and the rustic texture of the bread. This ciabatta is perfect for dipping in olive oil, pairing with cheeses, or making delicious sandwiches.

This Olive and Herb Ciabatta brings the delightful flavors of Mediterranean cuisine to your table. The combination of olives, fresh herbs, and a crusty exterior makes it a wonderful and versatile bread for various culinary occasions.

**Cheddar and Jalapeño Cornbread:**

Ingredients:

- 1 cup cornmeal
- 1 cup all-purpose flour
- 1 tablespoon baking powder
- 1/2 teaspoon baking soda
- 1/2 teaspoon salt
- 1 cup buttermilk
- 2 large eggs
- 1/4 cup unsalted butter, melted
- 1 cup sharp cheddar cheese, shredded
- 2 jalapeños, seeds removed and finely chopped

Directions:

Preheat Oven:

Preheat your oven to 375°F (190°C). Grease a 9-inch square baking pan.

Mix Dry Ingredients:

2. In a large bowl, whisk together cornmeal, all-purpose flour, baking powder, baking soda, and salt.

Combine Wet Ingredients:

3. In another bowl, whisk together buttermilk, eggs, and melted butter.

Mix Wet and Dry Ingredients:

4. Pour the wet ingredients into the dry ingredients and stir until just combined. Do not overmix.

Add Cheese and Jalapeños:

5. Fold in the shredded cheddar cheese and chopped jalapeños into the batter.

Pour into Pan:

6. Pour the batter into the prepared baking pan, spreading it evenly.

Bake:

7. Bake in the preheated oven for 25-30 minutes, or until the cornbread is golden brown and a toothpick inserted into the center comes out clean.

Cool:

8. Allow the cornbread to cool in the pan for 10 minutes, then transfer it to a wire rack to cool completely.

Slice and Serve:

9. Once cooled, slice the Cheddar and Jalapeño Cornbread into squares or wedges. Serve it as a side dish with chili, soups, or enjoy it on its own.

Optional:

10. For an extra kick, you can drizzle honey over the sliced cornbread before serving.

This Cheddar and Jalapeño Cornbread is a savory and slightly spicy twist on the classic. The combination of sharp cheddar and jalapeños adds a flavorful kick, making it a perfect accompaniment to hearty dishes or a delicious snack on its own.

**Cranberry Walnut Artisan Bread:**

Ingredients:

*For the Dough:*

- 3 cups bread flour
- 1 1/2 teaspoons salt
- 2 1/4 teaspoons active dry yeast
- 1 1/4 cups lukewarm water (110°F/43°C)
- 2 tablespoons olive oil
- 1/4 cup honey
- 1/2 cup dried cranberries
- 1/2 cup chopped walnuts

*For the Topping:*

- 1/4 cup chopped walnuts
- Honey for drizzling

Directions:

Activate Yeast:

In a small bowl, combine lukewarm water and active dry yeast. Let it sit for 5-10 minutes until frothy.

Prepare Dough:

2. In a large mixing bowl, combine bread flour and salt. Add the activated yeast mixture, olive oil, and honey. Mix until a sticky dough forms.

Knead and Add Mix-ins:

3. Turn the dough out onto a floured surface and knead for about 8-10 minutes, or until it becomes smooth and elastic. During the last few minutes of kneading, incorporate dried cranberries and chopped walnuts into the dough.

First Rise:

4. Place the dough in a lightly oiled bowl, cover it with a clean kitchen towel, and let it rise in a warm place for about 1-2 hours, or until it doubles in size.

Shape Artisan Bread:

5. Preheat your oven to 425°F (218°C). Place a baking stone or inverted baking sheet inside to heat.

Turn the risen dough out onto a floured surface and shape it into a round or oval loaf.

Second Rise:

7. Cover the shaped dough with a kitchen towel and let it rise for an additional 30-45 minutes.

Topping:

8. Press additional chopped walnuts onto the top of the loaf.

Bake:

9. Carefully transfer the shaped and risen dough onto the preheated baking stone or sheet. Bake for 25-30 minutes, or until the bread is golden brown and sounds hollow when tapped.

Drizzle with Honey:

10. Once out of the oven, drizzle honey over the top of the warm bread for a sweet finish.

Cool:

11. Allow the Cranberry Walnut Artisan Bread to cool on a wire rack for at least 30 minutes before slicing.

Slice and Enjoy:

12. Slice the bread and savor the delightful combination of sweet cranberries, crunchy walnuts, and the natural sweetness from honey. This artisan bread is perfect for both sweet and savory pairings.

This Cranberry Walnut Artisan Bread is a festive and flavorful option, ideal for the holiday season or any time you crave a delicious and unique bread. The sweet-tartness of cranberries, the crunch of walnuts, and the touch of honey make it a delightful treat for your taste buds.

**Rosemary and Garlic No-Knead Bread:**

Ingredients:

*For the Dough:*

- 3 cups all-purpose flour
- 1 1/2 teaspoons salt
- 1/4 teaspoon active dry yeast
- 1 1/2 cups lukewarm water (110°F/43°C)

*For the Flavor Infusion:*

- 3 tablespoons olive oil
- 3 cloves garlic, minced
- 2 tablespoons fresh rosemary, finely chopped
- Additional olive oil for brushing

Directions:

Mix Dough:

> In a large mixing bowl, combine all-purpose flour, salt, and active dry yeast. Add lukewarm water and stir until a shaggy dough forms.
> Cover the bowl with plastic wrap and let it sit at room temperature for 12-18 hours. The dough will rise and become bubbly.

Prepare Infusion:

3. In a small pan, heat olive oil over medium heat. Add minced garlic and chopped rosemary. Cook for 1-2 minutes until fragrant. Remove from heat and let it cool.

> Once the dough has fermented, gently fold in the garlic and rosemary-infused oil into the dough, incorporating it evenly.

Second Rise:

5. Cover the bowl again and let the dough rise for an additional 2 hours. It will become puffy.

Preheat Oven:

6. Preheat your oven to 450°F (232°C). Place a Dutch oven (with lid) inside to heat.

Shape and Final Rise:

7. Turn the dough out onto a well-floured surface. Gently shape it into a round loaf. Cover with a kitchen towel and let it rise for 30 minutes while the oven preheats.

Bake:

8. Carefully transfer the risen dough into the preheated Dutch oven. You can place parchment paper at the bottom for easy removal.

> Score the top of the dough with a sharp knife, creating a decorative pattern.
> Put the lid on the Dutch oven and bake for 30 minutes. Then, remove the lid and continue baking for an additional 10-15 minutes until the bread is golden brown and has a crusty exterior.

Cool:

11. Allow the Rosemary and Garlic No-Knead Bread to cool in the Dutch oven for 10 minutes, then transfer it to a wire rack to cool completely.

Brush with Olive Oil:

12. Brush the top of the bread with additional olive oil for a shiny finish.

Slice and Enjoy:

13. Slice the bread and savor the aromatic blend of rosemary and garlic. This no-knead bread is perfect for serving with soups, salads, or enjoying on its own.

This Rosemary and Garlic No-Knead Bread is a rustic and flavorful option that requires minimal effort. The long fermentation time enhances the flavor, and the infusion of rosemary and garlic adds a delightful aroma. It's a great choice for those who love artisan-style bread without the need for extensive kneading.

**Sunflower Seed Whole Wheat Bread:**

Ingredients:

*For the Dough:*

- 2 1/2 cups whole wheat flour
- 1 cup bread flour
- 1 1/2 teaspoons salt
- 2 1/4 teaspoons active dry yeast
- 1 1/4 cups lukewarm water (110°F/43°C)
- 2 tablespoons honey
- 2 tablespoons olive oil
- 1/2 cup sunflower seeds (plus extra for topping)

Directions:

Activate Yeast:

In a small bowl, combine lukewarm water, honey, and active dry yeast. Let it sit for 5-10 minutes until frothy.

Prepare Dough:

2. In a large mixing bowl, combine whole wheat flour, bread flour, and salt. Add the activated yeast mixture and olive oil. Mix until a dough forms.

Knead and Add Sunflower Seeds:

3. Turn the dough out onto a floured surface and knead for about 8-10 minutes, or until it becomes smooth and elastic. During the last few minutes of kneading, incorporate sunflower seeds into the dough.

First Rise:

4. Place the dough in a lightly oiled bowl, cover it with a clean kitchen towel, and let it rise in a warm place for about 1-2 hours, or until it doubles in size.

Shape and Second Rise:

5. Preheat your oven to 375°F (190°C). Grease a bread pan.

Punch down the risen dough and shape it into a loaf. Place it in the greased bread pan.

Cover the pan with a kitchen towel and let the dough rise for an additional 30-45 minutes.

Brush with Water and Top with Sunflower Seeds:

8. Brush the top of the risen dough with water and sprinkle additional sunflower seeds over the surface.

Bake:

9. Bake the Sunflower Seed Whole Wheat Bread in the preheated oven for 30-35 minutes, or until it's golden brown and sounds hollow when tapped.

Cool:

10. Allow the bread to cool in the pan for 10 minutes, then transfer it to a wire rack.

Slice and Enjoy:

11. Slice the Sunflower Seed Whole Wheat Bread and enjoy the nutty flavor and crunch of sunflower seeds. This bread is perfect for sandwiches, toasting, or pairing with your favorite spreads.

This Sunflower Seed Whole Wheat Bread is a wholesome and nutritious option, combining the heartiness of whole wheat with the nutty crunch of sunflower seeds. It's a versatile bread that adds a delightful texture to your meals.

www.ingramcontent.com/pod-product-compliance
Lightning Source LLC
LaVergne TN
LVHW081555060526
838201LV00054B/1888